# JAPANESE
## VISUAL DICTIONARY

D0877054

Published by Collins
An imprint of HarperCollins Publishers
Westerhill Road
Bishopbriggs
Glasgow G64 2QT

First Edition 2019

10 9 8 7 6 5 4 3

© HarperCollins Publishers 2019

ISBN 978-0-00-829037-5

Collins® is a registered trademark of
HarperCollins Publishers Limited

Typeset by Jouve, India

Printed in China by RR Donnelley APS

## Acknowledgements

We would like to thank those authors and
publishers who kindly gave permission for
copyright material to be used in the Collins
Corpus. We would also like to thank Times
Newspapers Ltd for providing valuable data.

A catalogue record for this book is available
from the British Library

If you would like to comment on any aspect
of this book, please contact us at the given
address or online.
E-mail dictionaries@harpercollins.co.uk
 www.facebook.com/collinsdictionary
 @collinsdict

**MANAGING EDITOR**
Maree Airlie

**FOR THE PUBLISHER**
Gerry Breslin
Gina Macleod
Kevin Robbins
Robin Scrimgeour

**CONTRIBUTORS**
Tessa Carroll
Harumi Currie
Lauren Reid
Anna Stevenson

**TECHNICAL SUPPORT**
Claire Dimeo

# CONTENTS

4   INTRODUCTION

7   THE ESSENTIALS

19   TRANSPORT

51   IN THE HOME

75   AT THE SHOPS

121   DAY-TO-DAY

151   LEISURE

177   SPORT

201   HEALTH

229   PLANET EARTH

251   CELEBRATIONS AND FESTIVALS

259   INDEX

Whether you're on holiday or staying in Japan for a slightly longer period of time, your **Collins Visual Dictionary** is designed to help you find exactly what you need, when you need it. With over a thousand clear and helpful images, you can quickly locate the vocabulary you are looking for.

### FAST FOOD | ファーストフード

Burgers and other American-style food can be found across Japan, and are popular in various fast-food chains.

**2 YOU MIGHT SAY...**

I'd like to order, please.
注文おねがいします。
chūmon onegai shimasu.

Do you deliver?
配達してもらえますか。
haitatsu shite moraemasu ka?

**3 YOU MIGHT HEAR...**

Sit-in or takeaway?
お召し上がりですか。お持ち帰りですか。
o-meshiagari desu ka? o-mochikaeri desu ka?

Would you like anything else?
他にご注文は?
hoka ni go-chūmon wa?

**4 VOCABULARY**

| | | |
|---|---|---|
| food stall<br>屋台<br>yatai | drive-thru<br>ドライブスルー<br>doraibusurū | to order<br>注文する<br>chūmon suru |
| vendor<br>売り子<br>uriko | takeaway food<br>持ち帰り<br>mochikaeri | to deliver<br>配達する<br>haitatsu suru |

**5 YOU SHOULD KNOW...**

More traditional Japanese fast food ranges from a quick bowl of noodles to sushi and pot noodles from convenience stores.

bento box
(お)弁当
(o)bentō

burger
バーガー
bāgā

chicken yakitori
焼き鳥
yakitori

133

4

**The Visual Dictionary includes:**

- 10 **chapters** arranged thematically, so that you can easily find what you need to suit the situation
- **1** **images** – illustrating essential items
- **2** **YOU MIGHT SAY...** – common phrases that you might want to use
- **3** **YOU MIGHT HEAR...** – common phrases that you might come across
- **4** **VOCABULARY** – common words that you might need
- **5** **YOU SHOULD KNOW...** – tips about local customs or etiquette
- an **index** to find all images quickly and easily
- essential **phrases** and **numbers** listed on the flaps for quick reference

## USING YOUR COLLINS VISUAL DICTIONARY

The points below explain a few basic concepts of Japanese pronunciation and grammar and will help ensure that your **Collins Visual Dictionary** gives you as much help as possible when using Japanese:

1) There are several systems for writing Japanese in Roman characters, but the most understandable for English speakers is called the Hepburn system, which has been adapted slightly for use in this dictionary. Long vowels (pronounced with twice the length of normal vowels) have been written with a bar over the top, except for the double i:

  > ā  ii  ē  ō  ū
  >
  > bus stop  バス停  basu-tē
  > street  通り  tōri

2) Japanese grammar is simple in many ways compared to European languages: there is no gender and there are no definite or indefinite articles; there is no difference between singular and plural; and verbs only have past and non-past (present or future) forms and do not change according to who is performing an action.

3) There are different levels of politeness in Japanese, but polite forms suitable for general use have been used in the phrases in this book.

  Verbs are shown in the "plain" form. This is the form used among family members and close friends, and to form more complex structures, so you may hear people using it. However, it is safest to stick to using the polite form to avoid appearing over-familiar or rude. In the polite form, Japanese verbs end in "-masu". Negative forms and past tenses are made by changing the verb ending.

4) Japanese uses small words called particles to show how different parts of the sentence relate to each other. Some are similar to English prepositions, but in Japanese they come immediately after the nouns they refer to. These particles have the following functions:

| | |
|---|---|
| wa | topic marker |
| ga | subject marker |
| o | direct object marker |
| ni | indirect object marker, goal and location marker |
| to | connects nouns, 'and' or 'with' |
| de | indicates by which means an action is carried out or where an action takes place |
| no | indicates that the second noun is described in some way by the first, e.g. possession |
| mo | "also/as well" |
| kara | "from/since" |
| made | "until/as far as" |

Other particles occur at the end of sentences to change the meaning from a straightforward statement. The most common ones are:

| | |
|---|---|
| ka | question marker |
| ne | asks for agreement or confirmation |
| yo | adds emphasis |

Finally, some particles are used to link clauses to make more complex sentences. Two of the most useful are **kara** "because/so" (which always comes after the reason or cause) and **ga** "but/although".

5) Japanese word order is *subject – object – verb*, with the verb at the end of the sentence. The basic Japanese sentence has a topic and a comment section. The topic, indicated by the topic marker **wa**, usually comes at the beginning of the sentence, but if it is understood among the speakers or from the context, it is often omitted. Personal pronouns are avoided; instead, the person's name is normally used, even for "you". The most neutral order for additional phrases in longer sentences is *time – manner – place*.

**FREE AUDIO**

We have created a free audio resource to help you learn and practise the Japanese words for all of the images shown in this dictionary. The Japanese words in each chapter are spoken by native speakers, giving you the opportunity to listen to each word twice and repeat it yourself. Download the audio from the website below to learn all of the vocabulary you need for communicating in Japanese.

**www.collinsdictionary.com/resources**

## THE ESSENTIALS | 必須事項

Whether you're going to be visiting Japan, or even living there, you'll want to be able to chat with people and get to know them better. Being able to communicate effectively with acquaintances, friends, family, and colleagues is key to becoming more confident in Japanese in a variety of everyday situations.

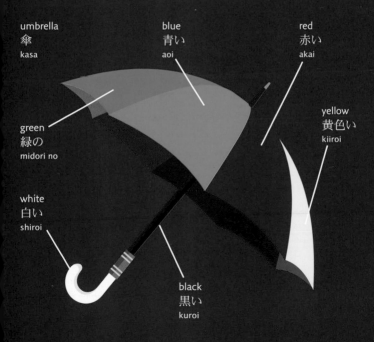

umbrella
傘
kasa

blue
青い
aoi

red
赤い
akai

green
緑の
midori no

yellow
黄色い
kiiroi

white
白い
shiroi

black
黒い
kuroi

Hello.
こんにちは。
konnichiwa.

Good evening.
こんばんは
konbanwa.

See you tomorrow.
また、明日。
mata, ashita.

Good morning.
おはよう(ございます)。
ohayō (gozaimasu).

Good night.
おやすみ(なさい)
oyasumi (nasai).

Goodbye.
さようなら
sayōnara.

Good afternoon.
こんにちは。
konnichiwa.

See you soon.
じゃあ、また。
jā, mata.

Bye!
じゃあね。
jā ne.

**YOU SHOULD KNOW...**

Japanese people bow to express their respect and appreciation. People bow to accompany greetings, words of appreciation, or apologies. The strength of the respect, gratitude, or apology dictates how low your bow should be.

There are two other common ways of saying goodbye in Japanese. The first, いってきます itte kimasu, is said by someone who is leaving but will return later. The second, いってらっしゃい itte rasshai, is said by the other person in response to that and literally means "go and return".

Yes.
はい。
hai.

No, thanks.
いいえ、結構です。
iie, kekkō desu.

OK!
はい!
hai!

No.
いいえ。
iie.

Excuse me.
すみません。
sumimasen.

Thank you.
ありがとう(ございます)。
arigatō (gozaimasu).

I don't know/
understand.
分かりません。
wakarimasen.

Sorry?
何ですか。
nan desu ka?

You're welcome.
いいえ(どういたしまして)。
iie (dō itashimashite).

please
お願いします。
onegai shimasu.

I'm sorry.
すみません。
sumimasen.

Go ahead./Here you are.
どうぞ
dōzo

How old are you?
何歳ですか。
nan-sai desu ka?

May I ask how old you are?
お年を聞いてもいいですか。
o-toshi o kiite mo ii desu ka?

When is your birthday?
誕生日はいつですか。
tanjōbi wa itsu desu ka?

I'm ... years old.
…歳です。
...sai desu.

My birthday is on...
誕生日は…です。
tanjōbi wa ...desu.

I was born in...
…で生まれました。
...de umaremashita.

Where are you from?
出身はどちらですか。
shusshin wa dochira desu ka?

Where do you live?
どこに住んでいますか。
doko ni sunde imasu ka?

I'm from...
私は…から来ました。
watashi wa ... kara kimashita.

I live in...
…に住んでいます。
...ni sunde imasu.

I'm...
私は…です。
watashi wa    desu.

Scottish
スコットランド人
sukottorando-jin

English
イングランド人
ingurando-jin

Irish
アイルランド人
airurando-jin

Welsh
ウェールズ人
wēruzu-jin

British
イギリス人
igirisu-jin

Are you married?
結婚していますか。
kekkon shite imasu ka?

I have a partner.
パートナーがいます。
pātonā ga imasu.

I'm single.
独身です。
dokushin desu.

I'm married.
結婚しています。
kekkon shite imasu.

I'm divorced.
離婚しました。
rikon shimashita.

Do you have any children?
お子さんがいますか。
o-kosan ga imasu ka?

I have ... children.
子供が…人います。
kodomo ga ...nin imasu.

I don't have any children.
子供がいません。
kodomo ga imasen.

Different versions of words for family members are used depending on whether you are talking about your own family members (in-group) or someone else's (out-group). In the list below, the terms before the slash are for your own family members, and those after it are honorific terms used to refer to someone else's. Usage is changing, however: younger people today sometimes use the honorific terms to talk about their own family.

Mr/Mrs/Miss/Ms
…さん
…san

husband
夫／ご主人
otto/go-shujin

wife
妻／奥さん
tsuma/oku-san

boyfriend
ボーイフレンド
bōi furendo

girlfriend
ガールフレンド
gāru furendo

partner
パートナー
pātonā

fiancé/fiancée
フィアンセ
fianse

son
息子／息子さん
musuko/musuko-san

daughter
娘／娘さん
musume/musume-san

mother
母／お母さん
haha/okā-san

father
父／お父さん
chichi/otō-san

older brother
兄／お兄さん
ani/onii-san

younger brother
弟／弟さん
otōto/otōto-san

older sister
姉／お姉さん
ane/onē-san

younger sister
妹／妹さん
imōto/imōto-san

uncle
おじ／おじさん
oji/oji-san

aunt
おば／おばさん
oba/oba-san

nephew
甥／甥ごさん
oi/oigo-san

niece
姪／姪ごさん
mē/mēgo-san

cousin
いとこ
itoko

grandfather
祖父／おじいさん
sofu/ojii-san

grandmother
祖母／おばあさん
sobo/obā-san

grandson
孫（息子）／お孫さ
ん
mago(musuko)/
omago-san

granddaughter
孫娘／孫娘さん
magomusume/
magomusume-san

stepfather
血の繋がらない父
chi no tsunagaranai
chichi

in-laws
義理の親戚
giri no shinseki

mother-in-law
義母
gibo

father-in-law
義父
gifu

daughter-in-law
義理の娘／…娘さ
ん
giri no musume/
…musume-san

son-in-law
義理の息子／…息
子さん
giri no musuko/
…musuko-san

brother-in-law
義理の兄弟
giri no kyōdai

sister-in-law
義理の姉妹
giri no shimai

friend
友達
tomodachi

neighbour
近所の人
kinjo no hito

baby
赤ん坊／赤ちゃん
akanbō/akachan

child/children
子供／お子さん
kodomo/o-ko-san

teenager
ティーンエージャー
tiin'ējā

parents
両親／ご両親
ryōshin/go-ryōshin

siblings
兄弟／ご兄弟
kyōdai/go-kyōdai

This is/These are…
こちらは…です。
kochira wa … desu.

This is my husband.
こちらは夫です。
kochira wa otto desu.

---

**YOU SHOULD KNOW…**

When speaking to family members, the honorific terms are used, except for younger brother/sister, when name + さん san, or more familiarly ちゃん chan (for boys and girls) or 君 kun (for boys) are used.

How are you?
お元気ですか。
o-genki desu ka?

How's it going?
最近、いかがですか。
saikin, ikaga desu ka?

Very well, thanks, and you?
元気です。…さんは?
genki desu. …san wa?

Fine, thanks.
ありがとう。元気です。
arigatō. genki desu.

Great!
すごく元気です。
sugoku genki desu.

Not bad, thanks.
ありがとう。まあまあです。
arigatō. māmā desu.

Could be worse.
まずまずです。
mazumazu desu.

I'm fine.
大丈夫です。
daijōbu desu.

I'm tired.
疲れました。
tsukaremashita.

I'm hungry.
お腹が減っています。
onaka ga hette imasu.

I'm thirsty.
のどが渇いています。
nodo ga kawaite imasu.

I'm cold.
寒いです。
samui desu.

I'm warm.
あたたかいです。
atatakai desu.

I'm hot.
あついです。
atsui desu.

I am/feel...
（私は）…
(watashi wa) ....

happy
うれしいです
ureshii desu

excited
わくわくします
wakuwaku shimasu

surprised
びっくりしました
bikkuri shimashita

annoyed
イライラしています
iraira shite imasu

angry
怒っています
okotte imasu

sad
悲しいです
kanashii desu

worried
心配です
shinpai desu

afraid
怖いです
kowai desu

bored
退屈です
taikutsu desu

well
健康です
kenkō desu

unwell
気分が悪いです
kibun ga warui desu

better
よくなりました
yoku narimashita

worse
悪くなりました
waruku narimashita

Japanese people tend to say where they work, rather than the kind of work they do. Working for a major company at whatever level is prestigious.

Where do you work?
どこで働いていますか。
doko de hataraite imasu ka?

What's your occupation?
お仕事は何ですか。
o-shigoto wa nan desu ka?

Do you work/study?
働いて／勉強していますか。
hataraite/benkyō shite imasu.

I'm self-employed.
自営業です。
jiēgyō desu.

I'm unemployed.
失業中です。
shitsugyō-chū desu.

I'm at university.
大学で勉強しています。
daigaku de benkyō shite imasu.

I'm retired.
退職しました。
taishoku shimashita.

I'm not working.
無職です。
mushoku desu.

I'm travelling.
旅行中です。
ryokō-chū desu.

I work from home.
家で働いています。
uchi de hataraite imasu.

I work part-/full-time.
パート／常勤で働いています。
pāto/jōkin de hataraite imasu.

I work at/in...
…で働いています。
... de hataraite imasu.

I work in a bank.
銀行に勤めています。
ginkō ni tsutomete imasu.

business
商売
shōbai

company
会社
kaisha

factory
工場
kōjō

government
政府
sēfu

hospital
病院
byōin

hotel
ホテル
hoteru

office
事務所／会社
jimusho/kaisha

restaurant
レストラン
resutoran

school
学校
gakkō

shop
店
mise

I'm a/an...
私は…です。
watashi wa ... desu.

I work as a/an...
…の仕事をしてい
ます。
…no shigoto o shite imasu.

architect
建築家
kenchikuka

builder
建築業者／大工
kenchiku-gyōsha/daiku

chef
シェフ
shefu

civil servant
公務員
kōmuin

cleaner
清掃人
sēsō-nin

decorator
内装業者
naisō-gyōsha

dentist
歯医者
haisha

doctor
医者
isha

driver
運転手
untenshu

electrician
電気技師
denki-gishi

engineer
技師
gishi

firefighter
消防士
shōbōshi

IT worker
IT 技術者
aitii gijutsusha

journalist
ジャーナリスト
jānarisuto

lawyer
弁護士
bengoshi

mechanic
機械工
kikaikō

nurse
看護師
kangoshi

office worker
事務員
jimuin

plumber
配管工
haikankō

police officer
警察官
kēsatsukan

postal worker
郵便局員
yūbinkyokuin

sales assistant
店員
ten'in

teacher
教師／先生
kyōshi/sensē

vet
獣医
jūi

waiter/waitress
ウェイター／ウェイ
トレス
weitā/weitoresu

**YOU SHOULD KNOW...**

Male white-collar employees are called サラリーマン sarariiman (lit: salary man), while the term "OL" (from "office lady") is used to refer to women working in secretarial or office support roles. The word 会社員 kaisha-in ("company employee") can be used to refer to both male and female office workers.

| | | |
|---|---|---|
| morning<br>朝<br>asa | It's nine o'clock.<br>9時です。<br>ku-ji desu. | When...?<br>いつ…?<br>itsu ...? |
| afternoon<br>午後<br>gogo | It's ten past nine.<br>9時10分です。<br>ku-ji juppun desu. | ... in two minutes.<br>…2分で<br>...ni-fun de |
| evening<br>晩<br>ban | It's quarter past nine.<br>9時15分です。<br>ku-ji jūgo-fun desu. | ... in an hour.<br>…1時間で<br>...ichi-jikan de |
| night<br>夜<br>yoru | It's half past nine.<br>9時半です。<br>ku-ji han desu. | ... in quarter of/half an hour.<br>…15／30分で<br>...jūgo-fun/sanju-ppun de |
| midday<br>真昼<br>mahiru | It's twenty to ten.<br>9時40分です。<br>ku-ji yonjuppun desu. | early<br>早い<br>hayai |
| midnight<br>真夜中<br>mayonaka | It's quarter to ten.<br>9時45分です。<br>ku-ji yonjūgo-fun desu. | late<br>遅い<br>osoi |
| a.m.<br>午前<br>gozen | It's five to ten.<br>10時5分前です。<br>jū-ji go-fun mae desu. | soon<br>もうすぐ<br>mōsugu |
| p.m.<br>午後<br>gogo | It's 10 a.m.<br>午前10時です。<br>gozen jū-ji desu. | later<br>あとで<br>ato de |
| What time is it?<br>何時ですか。<br>nan-ji desu ka? | It's 5 p.m.<br>午後5時です。<br>gogo go-ji desu. | now<br>今<br>ima |

| Monday | Wednesday | Friday | Sunday |
|---|---|---|---|
| 月曜日 | 水曜日 | 金曜日 | 日曜日 |
| getsuyōbi | suiyōbi | kin'yōbi | nichiyōbi |

| Tuesday | Thursday | Saturday | |
|---|---|---|---|
| 火曜日 | 木曜日 | 土曜日 | |
| kayōbi | mokuyōbi | doyōbi | |

| January | April | July | October |
|---|---|---|---|
| 1月 | 4月 | 7月 | 10月 |
| ichigatsu | shigatsu | shichigatsu | jūgatsu |

| February | May | August | November |
|---|---|---|---|
| 2月 | 5月 | 8月 | 11月 |
| nigatsu | gogatsu | hachigatsu | jūichigatsu |

| March | June | September | December |
|---|---|---|---|
| 3月 | 6月 | 9月 | 12月 |
| sangatsu | rokugatsu | kugatsu | jūnigatsu |

| day | month | weekly |
|---|---|---|
| 日 | 月 | 週に1度（の） |
| hi | tsuki | shū ni ichi-do (no) |

| weekend | year | fortnightly |
|---|---|---|
| 週末 | 年 | 2週間に1度（の） |
| shūmatsu | toshi | ni-shūkan ni ichi-do (no) |

| week | decade | monthly |
|---|---|---|
| 週 | 10年間 | 月に1度（の） |
| shū | jū-nenkan | tsuki ni ichi-do (no) |

| fortnight | daily | yearly |
|---|---|---|
| 2週間 | 毎日（の） | 年に1度（の） |
| ni-shūkan | mainichi (no) | nen ni ichi-do (no) |

on Mondays
月曜日に
getsuyōbi ni

every Sunday
毎週日曜日
maishū nichiyōbi

last Thursday
先週の木曜日
senshū no mokuyōbi

next Friday
来週の金曜日
raishū no kin'yōbi

last week
先週
senshū

next week
来週
raishū

next month
来月
raigetsu

today
今日
kyō

tonight
今晩
konban

tomorrow
明日
ashita

yesterday
昨日
kinō

the day after tomorrow
あさって
asatte

the day before yesterday
おととい
ototoi

the week before
前の週
mae no shū

the week after
次の週
tsugi no shū

in February
2月に
nigatsu ni

in 2019
2019年に
nisenjūhkyū-nen ni

in the '80s
80年代に
hachijū-nen dai ni

What day is it today?
今日は何曜日ですか。
kyō wa nan'yōbi desu ka?

What is today's date?
今日は何日ですか。
kyō wa nan-nichi desu ka?

When is it?
いつですか。
itsu desu ka?

spring
春
haru

summer
夏
natsu

autumn
秋
aki

winter
冬
fuyu

in spring/summer/autumn/winter
春／夏／秋／冬に
haru/natsu/aki/fuyu ni

rainy season
梅雨
tsuyu

How's the weather?
天気はどうですか。
tenki wa dō desu ka?

What's the forecast for today/tomorrow?
今日／明日の天気予報はどうですか。
kyō/ashita no tenki-yohō wa dō desu ka?

Is it going to rain?
雨がふりそうですか。
ame ga furi sō desu ka?

What a lovely day!
いい天気ですね。
ii tenki desu ne.

What awful weather!
ひどい天気ですね。
hidoi tenki desu ne.

It's sunny/cloudy/stormy.
晴れて／くもって／荒れています。
harete/kumotte/arete imasu.

It's misty.
かすんでいます。
kasunde imasu.

It's foggy.
霧が深いです。
kiri ga fukai desu.

It's pleasantly cool.
涼しいです。
suzushii desu.

It's freezing.
すごく寒いです。
sugoku samui desu.

It's raining/snowing.
雨／雪 が降っています。
ame/yuki ga futte imasu.

It's windy.
風が強いです。
kaze ga tsuyoi desu.

It is...
天気は … です。
tenki wa ...desu.

nice
いい
ii

horrible
悪い
warui

hot
暑い
atsui

warm
暖かい
atatakai

cold
寒い
samui

wet
雨
ame

humid
蒸し暑い
mushiatsui

sun
太陽
taiyō

rain
雨
ame

snow
雪
yuki

hail
あられ
arare

ice
氷
kōri

wind
風
kaze

thunder
雷鳴
raimē

lightning
稲光
inabikari

# TRANSPORT | 交通

Japan has excellent public transport, from high-speed bullet trains to metro and buses. Bridges or tunnels now link the four main islands. Transport and roads are very busy around public holidays.

helicopter
ヘリコプター
herikoputā

rotor
ローター
rōtā

blade
ブレード
burēdo

cockpit
コックピット
kokkupitto

nose
機首
kishu

tail
尾部
bibu

Where is...?
…はどこですか。
...wa doko desu ka?

Which way is...?
…はどちらですか。
...wa dochira desu ka?

What's the quickest way to...?
…に行く一番早い方法は何ですか。
...ni iku ichiban hayai hōhō wa nan desu ka?

Is it far from here?
ここから遠いですか。
koko kara tōi desu ka?

I'm lost.
道に迷いました。
michi ni mayoimashita.

I'm looking for...
…を探しています。
...o sagashite imasu.

Can I walk there?
そこまで歩けますか。
soko made arukemasu ka?

Is there a bus/train to...?
…に行くバス／電車はありますか。
...ni iku basu/densha wa arimasu ka?

It's over there.
あそこですよ。
asoko desu yo.

It's ... minutes away.
ここから…分ぐらいです。
koko kara ... fun/pun gurai desu.

Go straight ahead.
まっすぐ行ってください。
massugu itte kudasai.

Turn left/right.
左に曲がってください。
hidari ni magatte kudasai.

It's next to...
…の隣です。
...no tonari desu.

It's opposite ...
…の向かいです。
...no mukai desu.

Follow the signs for...
…の表示に従ってください。
...no hyōji ni shitagatte kudasai.

street
通り
tōri

commuter
通勤する人
tsūkin suru hito

driver
運転手
untenshu

passenger
乗客
jōkyaku

pedestrian
歩行者
hokōsha

traffic
交通
kōtsū

traffic jam
交通渋滞
kōtsū jūtai

rush hour
ラッシュアワー
rasshuawā

public transport
公共交通機関
kōkyō kōtsū kikan

route
道順
michijun

road sign
道路標識
dōro hyōshiki

to walk
歩く
aruku

to drive
運転する
unten suru

to return
帰る／戻る
kaeru/modoru

to cross
横切る
yokogiru

to turn
曲がる
magaru

to commute
通勤する
tsūkin suru

to ask for/give directions
行き方を聞く／教える
ikikata o kiku/oshieru

map
地図
chizu

ticket
チケット／切符
chiketto/kippu

timetable
時刻表
jikokuhyō

Traffic drives on the left, as in the UK. You must get an international driving permit before leaving your country and you will need to show it to rent a car. You must also carry your own national driving licence while driving in Japan. All motorways are toll roads.

## YOU MIGHT SAY...

Is this the road to...?
…に行くのはこの道ですか。
…ni iku no wa kono michi desu ka?

Can I park here?
ここに駐車してもいいですか。
koko ni chūsha shite mo ii desu ka?

Do I have to pay to park?
駐車するのに料金がかかりますか。
chūsha suru no ni ryōkin ga kakarimasu ka?

Where can I hire a car?
どこで車を借りられますか。
doko de kuruma ga kariraremasu ka?

I'd like to hire a car...
…車を借りたいんですが。
…kuruma o karitai n desu ga.

... for four days.
4日間
yokkakan

... for a week.
1週間
isshūkan

What is your daily/weekly rate?
1日／1週間、いくらですか。
ichinichi/isshūkan ikura desu ka?

When/Where must I return it?
いつ／どこに車を返さなければいけませんか。
itsu/doko ni kuruma o kaesanakereba ikemasen ka?

Where is the nearest petrol station?
一番近いガソリンスタンドはどこですか。
ichiban chikai gasorin-sutando wa doko desu ka?

I'd like ... yen worth of fuel, please.
…円分、入れてください。
... en bun irete kudasai.

I'd like ... litres of fuel, please.
…リットル、入れてください。
…rittoru irete kudasai.

It's pump number...
…番の給油機です。
…ban no kyūyuki desu.

You can/can't park here.
ここに駐車できます／できません。
koko ni chūsha dekimasu/dekimasen.

It's free to park here.
駐車は無料です。
chūsha wa muryō desu.

It costs ... to park here.
ここの駐車料は…円です。
koko no chūsharyō wa ...en desu.

Car hire is ... per day/week.
レンタカーは1日／1週間…です。
rentakā wa ichinichi/isshūkan ... desu.

May I see your documents, please?
書類を見せてください。
shurui o misete kudasai.

Please return it to...
…に返してください。
...ni kaeshite kudasai.

Please return the car with a full tank of fuel.
満タンにして車を返してください。
mantan ni shite kaeshite kudasai.

Which pump are you at?
何番の給油機ですか。
nan-ban no kyūyuki desu ka?

How much fuel would you like?
いくら分、入れましょうか。
ikura bun iremashō ka?

## VOCABULARY

| | | |
|---|---|---|
| people carrier<br>ワゴン車<br>wagonsha | back seat<br>後部座席<br>kōbuzaseki | engine<br>エンジン<br>enjin |
| motorhome<br>キャンピングカー<br>kyanpingukā | child seat<br>チャイルドシート<br>chairudo shiito | battery<br>バッテリー<br>batterii |
| passenger seat<br>助手席<br>joshuseki | roof rack<br>ルーフラック<br>rūfu rakku | brake<br>ブレーキ<br>burēki |
| driver's seat<br>運転席<br>untenseki | sunroof<br>サンルーフ<br>sanrūfu | accelerator<br>アクセル<br>akuseru |

clutch
クラッチ
kuratchi

air conditioning
空調
kūchō

cruise control
クルーズコントロール
kurūzu-kontorōru

exhaust (pipe)
排気管
haikikan

fuel tank
燃料タンク
nenryō tanku

gearbox
ギアボックス
giabokkusu

Breathalyser®
酒気検査機
shuki-kensaki

automatic
オートマ車
ōtomasha

electric car
電気自動車
denki jidōsha

hybrid
ハイブリッド車
haiburiddosha

to start the engine
エンジンをかける
enjin o kakeru

to brake
ブレーキをかける
burēki o kakeru

to overtake
追い越す
oikosu

to park
駐車する
chūsha suru

to reverse
バックする
bakku suru

to slow down
スピードを落とす
supiido o otosu

to speed
制限速度を超える
sēgen sokudo o koeru

to stop
止まる
tomaru

## INTERIOR

dashboard
ダッシュボード
dasshubōdo

fuel gauge
燃料計
nenryōkē

gearstick
シフトレバー
shifutorebā

glove compartment
グローブボックス
gurōbu bokkusu

handbrake
サイドブレーキ
saidoburēki

headrest
ヘッドレスト
heddo resuto

ignition
イグニッション
igunisshon

rearview mirror
バックミラー
bakkumirā

sat nav
カーナビ
kānabi

seatbelt
シートベルト
shiito beruto

speedometer
速度計
sokudokē

steering wheel
ハンドル
handoru

boot
トランク
toranku

roof
屋根
yane

door
ドア
doa

window
窓
mado

wing
フェンダー
fendā

wheel
車輪
sharin

tyre
タイヤ
taiya

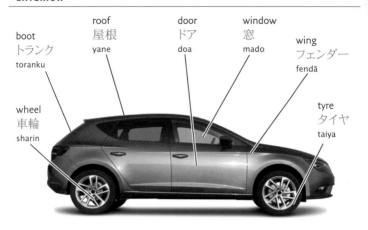

windscreen
フロントガラス
furonto garasu

windscreen wiper
ワイパー
waipā

wing mirror
サイドミラー
saido mirā

bonnet
ボンネット
bonnetto

bumper
バンパー
banpā

number plate
ナンバープレート
nanbā purēto

headlight
ヘッドライト
heddoraito

indicator
方向指示器
hōkō shijiki

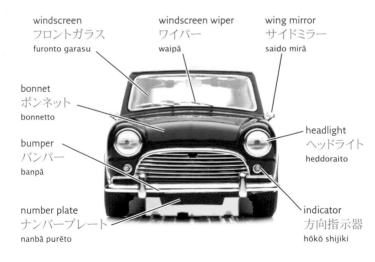

## VOCABULARY

single-track road
両側一車線道路
ryōgawa isshasen dōro

corner
曲がり角
magarikado

exit
出口
deguchi

slip road
高速道路の進入退
出路
kōsokudōro no shinnyū-
taishutsuro

layby
待避所
taihijo

parking meter
パーキングメーター
pākingu mētā

speed limit
制限速度
sēgen sokudo

diversion
う回路
ukairo

no entry
進入禁止
shinnyū kinshi

driving licence
運転免許証
unten menkyoshō

car registration
document
車両登録証
sharyō tōrokushō

car insurance
自動車保険
jidōsha hoken

car hire/rental
レンタカー
rentakā

unleaded petrol
無鉛ガソリン
muen gasorin

diesel
ディーゼル／軽油
diizeru/kēyu

## YOU SHOULD KNOW...

Speed limits in Japan are in kmph and lower than in the UK. The limits are:
40 kmph in urban areas and 30 kmph in side streets; 100 or 120 kmph on
motorways (with minimum speeds of 40 or 50 kmph); and 50 or 60 kmph
elsewhere. There is zero tolerance of drinking and driving.

accessible parking space
身障者用駐車スペー
ス
shinshōsha yō chūsha supēsu

bridge
橋
hashi

car park
駐車場
chūshajō

car wash
洗車
sensha

fuel pump
給油機
kyūyuki

junction
交差点
kōsaten

lane
車線
shasen

level crossing
踏切
fumikiri

motorway/toll road
高速道路
kōsoku-dōro

parking space
駐車スペース
chūsha supēsu

pavement
歩道
hodō

pedestrian crossing
横断歩道
ōdan-hodō

petrol station
ガソリンスタンド
gasorin sutando

police officer
警察官
kēsatsukan

road
道路
dōro

roadworks
工事中
kōjichū

roundabout
環状交差点
kanjō kōsaten

speed camera
スピードカメラ
supiido kamera

toll point
料金所
ryōkinjo

traffic cone
ロードコーン
rōdokōn

traffic lights
信号
shingō

tunnel
トンネル
tonneru

If you break down, the emergency telephone number for the Japanese equivalent of the AA (JAF – Japan Automobile Federation) is 0570-00-8139 or # 8139. If you have an accident, call the police on 110 or ambulance/ fire service on 119.

## YOU MIGHT SAY...

Can you help me?
手伝ってもらえませんか。
tetsudatte moraemasen ka?

I've broken down.
車が故障しました。
kuruma ga koshō shimashita.

I've had an accident.
事故を起こしました。
jiko o okoshimashita.

I've run out of petrol.
ガス欠です。
gasuketsu desu.

I've got a flat tyre.
パンクしました。
panku shimashita.

I've lost my car keys.
車の鍵を失くしました。
kuruma no kagi o nakushimashita.

The car won't start.
車が動きません。
kuruma ga ugokimasen.

There's a problem with...
…に問題があります。
...ni mondai ga arimasu.

I've been injured.
けがをしました。
kega o shimashita.

Is there a garage/petrol station nearby?
近くに修理工場／ガソリンスタンドがありますか。
chikaku ni shūri-kōjō/gasorin-sutando ga arimasu ka?

Can you tow me to a garage?
修理工場まで牽引してもらえますか。
shūri-kōjō made ken'in shite moraemasu ka?

How much will a repair cost?
修理にいくらぐらいかかりますか。
shūri ni ikura gurai kakarimasu ka?

When will the car be fixed?
車はいつ直りますか。
kuruma wa itsu naorimasu ka?

May I take your insurance details?
保険の詳細を教えてください。
hoken no shōsai o oshiete kudasai.

## YOU MIGHT HEAR...

Do you need any help?
手伝いましょうか。
tetsudaimashō ka?

Are you hurt?
けがをしませんでしたか。
kega o shimasen deshita ka?

What's wrong with your car?
車がどこかおかしいですか。
kuruma ga dokoka okashii desu ka?

Where have you broken down?
どこで故障していますか。
doko de koshō shite imasu ka?

I can tow you to...
…まで牽引してあげますよ。
...made ken'in shite agemasu yo.

I can give you a jumpstart.
私の車のバッテリーにつなぎ
ましょう。
watashi no kuruma no batterii ni
tsunagimashō.

The repairs will cost...
修理は…円ぐらいかかりま
す。
shūri wa ...en gurai kakarimasu.

We need to order new parts.
新しい部品を注文しなければ
なりません。
atarashii buhin o chūmon shinakereba
narimasen.

The car will be ready by...
車は…までにお渡しできま
す。
kuruma wa ... made ni o-watashi
dekimasu.

I need your insurance details.
保険の詳細を教えてくださ
い。
hoken no shōsai o oshiete kudasai.

## VOCABULARY

| | | |
|---|---|---|
| accident | flat tyre | to have a flat tyre |
| 事故 | パンクしたタイヤ | パンクしている |
| jiko | panku shita taiya | panku shite iru |
| breakdown | to break down | to change a tyre |
| 故障 | 故障する | タイヤを換える |
| koshō | koshō suru | taiya o kaeru |
| collision | to have an accident | to tow |
| 衝突 | 事故を起こす | 牽引する |
| shōtotsu | jiko o okosu | ken'in suru |

airbag
エアバッグ
eabaggu

antifreeze
不凍液
futōeki

emergency phone
非常電話
hijō denwa

garage
修理工場
shūri kōjō

hi-viz vest
安全反射ベスト
anzen hansha besuto

jack
ジャッキ
jakki

jump leads
ブースターケーブル
būsutā kēburu

mechanic
修理工
shūrikō

snow chains
タイヤチェーン
taiya chēn

spare wheel
予備タイヤ
yobi taiya

tow truck
レッカー車
rekkāsha

warning triangle
三角警告板
sankaku kēkokuban

Taxis may be the most convenient way to get around in Japan. Tipping is not customary, but you may tell the driver to keep the change if it's a small amount.

### YOU MIGHT SAY...

To ..., please.
…までお願いします。
...made onegai shimasu.

How much is it?
いくらですか。
ikura desu ka?

Please let me out here.
こで降ろしてください。
koko de oroshite kudasai.

Please keep the change.
おつりは取っておいてください。
otsuri wa totte oite kudasai.

### YOU MIGHT HEAR...

It takes about...
…ぐらい、かかります。
...gurai, kakarimasu.

That comes to ... yen.
…円です。
...en desu.

### VOCABULARY

taxi rank
タクシーのりば
takushii noriba

vacant
空車
kūsha

to book a taxi
タクシーを予約する
takushii o yoyaku suru

fare meter
料金メーター
ryōkin mētā

in use
実車
jissha

to call a taxi
タクシーを呼ぶ
takushii o yobu

automatic door
自動ドア
jidō-doa

driver
運転手
untenshu

taxi
タクシー
takushii

Long-distance buses are cheaper than trains. Tickets are sold at bus terminals or Japan Railways railway stations (for JR buses). Trams still run in some cities, for example, Sapporo and Hiroshima.

## YOU MIGHT SAY...

Which bus goes to the city centre?
どのバスが町の中心に行きますか。
dono basu ga machi no chūshin ni ikimasu ka?

Where is the bus/tram stop?
バス停／市電乗り場はどこですか。
basu-tē/shiden-noriba wa doko desu ka?

Which stand does the coach leave from?
長距離バスはどの乗り場から出ますか。
chōkyori basu wa dono noriba kara demasu ka?

How frequent are buses to...?
…行きのバスはどれぐらいの間隔で出ますか。
...iki no basu wa dore gurai no kankaku de demasu ka?

Where can I buy tickets?
どこで切符が買えますか。
doko de kippu ga kaemasu ka?

Can I buy a ticket on the bus/tram?
バス／市電で切符が買えますか。
basu/shiden de kippu ga kaemasu ka?

How much is it to go to...?
…に行くのはいくらですか。
...ni iku no wa ikura desu ka?

A single/return ticket, please.
片道／往復切符をお願いします。
katamichi/ōfuku kippu o onegai shimasu.

Could you tell me when to get off?
どこで降りたらいいか教えていただけますか。
doko de oritara ii ka oshiete kudasai.

How many stops is it?
いくつ目で降りたらいいですか。
ikutsume de oritara ii desu ka?

I want to get off at the next stop, please.
すみません、次で降ります。
sumimasen. tsugi de orimasu.

The number 17 goes to...
17番は…に行きます。
jūnana-ban wa ... ni ikimasu.

You can/can't buy tickets on the bus.
バスで切符が買えます／買えません。
basu de kippu ga kaemasu/kaemasen.

The bus stop is down the road.
バス停はこの道の先です。
basu-tē wa kono michi no saki desu.

You buy tickets at the machine/office.
券売機／窓口で切符を買ってください。
kenbaiki/madoguchi de katte kudasai.

It leaves from stand 21.
21番から出ます。
nijūichi-ban kara demasu.

There's a bus every 10 minutes.
バスは10分おきに出ます。
basu wa juppun oki ni demasu.

This is your stop, sir/madam.
ここで降りてください。
koko de orite kudasai.

## YOU SHOULD KNOW...

Passengers usually board local buses via the rear door, and take a boarding ticket (整理券 sēriken) from the machine there. The display at the front of the bus shows the fares for the next stop according to the numbers on the tickets. Drop the exact fare (using the change machine if necessary) and boarding ticket into the box by the driver when you leave the bus at the front. On some buses, passengers board at the front, pay a flat fare and get off at the rear. Multijourney discounted tickets (回数券 kaisūken) are often available, as are day passes (1日乗車券 ichinichi jōshaken) in popular tourist destinations.

## VOCABULARY

bus route
バス路線
basu rosen

tram stop
市電乗り場
shiden-noriba

child's fare
子供料金
kodomo ryōkin

bus lane
バスレーン
basu-rēn

fare
運賃
unchin

wheelchair access
車椅子での乗車
kuruma-isu de no jōsha

bus pass
バス定期
basu tēki

full fare
全額料金
zengaku ryōkin

night bus
深夜バス
shin'ya basu

shuttle bus
シャトルバス
shatoru basu

school bus
スクールバス
sukūru basu

to catch the bus
バスに乗る
basu ni noru

airport bus
空港バス
kūkō basu

tour bus
観光バス
kankō basu

to stop the bus
バスを止める
basu o tomeru

bus
バス
basu

bus station
バスターミナル
basu tāminaru

bus stop
バス停
basu-tē

bus ticket
チケット／切符
chiketto/kippu

buzzer
降車ブザー
kōsha buzā

coach
長距離バス
chōkyori basu

minibus
マイクロバス
maikuro basu

sightseeing bus
観光バス
kankō basu

tram
市電／路面電車
shiden/romen-densha

## VOCABULARY

motorcyclist
オートバイに乗る
人
ōtobai ni noru hito

moped
原付
gentsuki

scooter
スクーター
sukūtā

fuel tank
燃料タンク
nenryō tanku

handlebars
ハンドル
handoru

mudguard
泥よけ
doro yoke

kickstand
キックスタンド
kikkusutando

exhaust pipe
排気管
haikikan

leathers
レザースーツ
rezā sūtsu

boots
ブーツ
būtsu

crash helmet
フルフェイス・ヘル
メット
furufēsu herumetto

knee protectors
膝プロテクター
hiza–protekutā

leather gloves
レザーグローブ
rezā gurōbu

leather jacket
レザージャケット
rezā jaketto

motorbike
オートバイ
ōtobai

Bicycles are widely used in Japan and can be hired in many tourist areas. Although people are supposed to cycle on the road, they mainly ride on the pavement in towns and cities. Helmets are not compulsory.

### YOU MIGHT SAY...

Where can I hire a bicycle?
どこで自転車を借りられますか。
doko de jitensha o kariraremasu ka?

How much is it to hire?
借りるのはいくらですか。
kariru no wa ikura desu ka?

My bike has a puncture.
自転車がパンクしました。
jitensha ga panku shimashita.

Could you lend me a bicycle pump?
空気入れを貸してください。
kūki-ire o kashite kudasai.

### YOU MIGHT HEAR...

Bike hire is ... per day.
自転車を借りるのは1日につき…です。
jitensha o kariru no wa ichinichi ni tsuki ...desu.

There's a cycle path from ... to...
…から...まで自転車専用道路があります。
...kara ...made jitensha sen'yō dōro ga arimasu.

### VOCABULARY

cyclist
自転車に乗る人
jitensha ni noru hito

mountain bike
マウンテンバイク
maunten baiku

road bike
ロードバイク
rōdo baiku

bike hire
レンタサイクル
renta saikuru

bike rack
自転車ラック
jitensha rakku

cycle path
自転車道路
jitensha dōro

puncture
パンク
panku

to get a puncture
パンクする
panku suru

to cycle
自転車に乗る
jitensha ni noru

### YOU SHOULD KNOW...

Japan's strict laws on drink-driving also apply to riding a bike.

bell
ベル
beru

bike lock
自転車ロック
jitensha rokku

front light
ヘッドランプ
heddoranpu

helmet
ヘルメット
herumetto

pump
空気入れ
kūki-ire

reflector
リフレクター
rifurekutā

## BICYCLE

| handlebars | gears | crossbar | saddle | frame |
|---|---|---|---|---|
| ハンドル | ギア | トップチューブ | サドル | フレーム |
| handoru | gia | toppuchūbu | sadoru | furēmu |

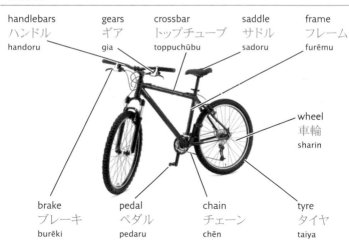

wheel
車輪
sharin

brake
ブレーキ
burēki

pedal
ペダル
pedaru

chain
チェーン
chēn

tyre
タイヤ
taiya

Japan has an extensive rail network, run by the Japan Railways (JR) group and many smaller private railway companies with their own lines in the major conurbations. Trains are now generally non-smoking but there are still standing smoking cabins on some bullet trains. Tickets are made up of a basic fare based on distance (乗車券 jōshaken), plus supplements for limited express (特急 tokkyū), express (急行 kyūkō) and high-speed bullet trains (新幹線 shinkansen); reservations are recommended for high-speed trains.

**YOU MIGHT SAY...**

When is the next train to...?
…に行く次の電車はいつです
か。
...ni iku tsugi no densha wa itsu desu
ka?

Where is the nearest metro station?
一番近い地下鉄の駅はどこで
すか。
ichiban chikai chikatetsu no eki wa
doko desu ka?

Which platform does it leave from?
どのホームから出ますか。
dono hōmu kara demasu ka?

A ticket to ..., please.
…までの切符をお願いします。
...made no kippu o onegai shimasu.

I'd like to reserve a seat, please.
指定席をお願いします。
shitē-seki o onegai shimasu.

Do I have to change?
電車を乗り換えなければいけ
ませんか。
densha o norikaenakereba ikemasen ka?

Where do I change for...?
…に行くのにはどこで乗り換
えなければいけませんか。
...ni iku no ni wa doko de
norikaenakereba ikemasen ka?

Where is platform 4?
4番線はどこですか。
yon-bansen wa doko desu ka?

Is this the right platform for...?
…行きはこのホームでいいで
すか。
...iki wa kono hōmu de ii desu ka?

Is this the train for...?
この電車は…に行きますか。
kono densha wa ...ni ikimasu ka?

Is this seat free?
この席は空いていますか。
kono seki wa aite imasu ka?

I've missed my train!
電車に乗り遅れました。
densha ni noriokuremashita.

The next train leaves at...
次の電車は…に出ます。
tsugi no densha wa ... ni demasu.

Would you like a single or return ticket?
片道ですか、往復ですか。
katamichi desu ka, ōfuku desu ka?

You must change at...
…でお乗り換えください。
...de o-norikae kudasai.

Platform 4 is down there.
4番線は向こうです。
yon-bansen wa mukō desu.

No, you have to go to platform 2.
いいえ、2番線に行ってください。
iie, ni-bansen ni itte kudasai.

This seat is free/taken.
この席は空いています／座っている人がいます。
kono seki wa aite imasu/suwatte iru hito ga imasu.

The next stop is...
次の停車駅は…です。
tsugi no tēsha eki wa ...desu.

Change here for...
…へはここでお乗り換えください。
...ewa koko de o-norikae kudasai.

You can't travel on this train without an express ticket.
特急券がなければ乗れません。
tokkyūken ga nakereba noremasen.

## YOU SHOULD KNOW...

The major cities all have metro systems, running from around 5 a.m. to midnight. Tokyo's metro system is one of the largest and busiest in the world.

## VOCABULARY

| | | |
|---|---|---|
| railcard<br>レールカード<br>rērukādo | metro station<br>地下鉄の駅<br>chikatetsu no eki | local/express train<br>普通/急行（列車）<br>futsū/kyūkō (ressha) |
| line<br>線<br>sen | left luggage<br>手荷物預かり<br>tenimotsu azukari | passenger train<br>客車<br>kyakusha |

41

| goods train | single/return ticket | seat reservation |
|---|---|---|
| 貨物列車 | 片道/往復切符 | 座席指定 |
| kamotsu ressha | katamichi/ōfuku kippu | zaseki shitē |
| train driver | e-ticket | non-smoking carriage |
| 電車の運転手 | Eチケット | 禁煙車 |
| densha no untenshu | ii chiketto | kin'en-sha |
| rail network | first-class | to change trains |
| 鉄道網 | グリーン車 | 電車を乗り換える |
| tetsudōmō | guriin-sha | densha o norikaeru |

**YOU SHOULD KNOW...**

Bento boxes (弁当 bentō) – boxed lunches made with seasonal local ingredients – are sold at stations and on long-distance trains. The seller will bow on entering the carriage with a trolley and will announce that he/she is selling in this carriage now: 車内販売でございます。(shanai hanbai de gozaimasu).

boxed lunch
駅弁
eki-ben

bullet train
新幹線
shinkansen

carriage/coach
客車／車両
kyakusha/sharyō

information board
掲示板
kējiban

locomotive
機関車
kikansha

luggage locker
コインロッカー
koin rokkā

luggage rack
網棚
amidana

metro
地下鉄
chikatetsu

monorail
モノレール
monorēru

platform
ホーム
hōmu

railway station
駅
eki

station staff
駅員
eki-in

ticket barrier
改札口
kaisatsu guchi

ticket collector
車掌
shashō

ticket machine
券売機
kenbaiki

ticket office
切符売場
kippu uriba

track
線路
senro

train
電車
densha

There are airports offering intercontinental flights in or near Tokyo, Osaka, Nagoya, and Fukuoka, as well as smaller regional airports offering international flights within Asia.

## YOU MIGHT SAY...

I'm looking for check-in/my gate.
チェックインカウンター／搭乗ゲートを探しています。
chekkuin-kauntā/tōjō-gēto o sagashite imasu.

I'm checking in one case.
スーツケースを一つチェックインします。
sūtsukēsu o hitotsu chekkuin shimasu.

Which gate does the plane leave from?
飛行機はどのゲートから出発しますか。
hikōki wa dono gēto kara shuppatsu shimasu ka?

When does the gate open/close?
いつ、ゲートは開きますか／閉まりますか。
itsu, gēto wa akimasu/shimarimasu ka?

Is the flight on time?
便は時間どおりですか。
bin wa jikan dōri desu ka?

I would like a window/aisle seat, please.
窓側／通路側の席がいいんですが。
mado/tsūro gawa no seki ga ii n desu ga.

I've lost my luggage.
荷物を失くしました。
nimotsu o nakushimashita.

My luggage hasn't arrived.
荷物が着きません。
nimotsu ga todokimasen.

My flight has been delayed.
飛行機が遅れています。
hikōki ga okurete imasu.

I've missed my connecting flight.
乗り継ぎ便を逃しました。
noritsugi-bin o nogashimashita.

Is there a shuttle bus service?
シャトルバスがありますか。
shatoru-basu ga arimasu ka?

May I see your ticket/passport, please?
チケット／パスポートを見せていただけますか。
chiketto/pasupōto o misete itadakemasu ka.

Your flight is on time/delayed/cancelled.
便は時間どおりです／遅れています／キャンセルになりました。
bin wa jikan dōri desu/okurete imasu/kyanseru ni narimashita.

How many bags are you checking in?
チェックインするお荷物はいくつですか。
chekkuin suru o-nimotsu wa ikutsu desu ka?

Is this your bag?
これはお客様のお荷物ですか。
kore wa o-kyakusama no o-nimotsu desu ka?

Your luggage exceeds the maximum weight.
お荷物が重量制限を超えています。
o-nimotsu ga jūryō-sēgen o koete imasu.

Flight ... is now ready for boarding.
…便の搭乗を開始いたします。
...bin no tōjō o kaishi itashimasu.

Last call for passenger...
…様、最後のお呼び出しをいたします。
...sama, saigo no o-yobidashi o itashimasu.

Please go to gate number...
…番ゲートにいらっしゃってください。
...ban gēto ni irasshatte kudasai.

## VOCABULARY

seaplane
水上飛行機
suijō-hikōki

airline
航空会社
kōkūgaisha

flight
便
bin

terminal
発着ロビー／ターミナル
hatchaku biru/tāminaru

Arrivals/Departures
到着/出発
tōchaku/shuppatsu

security
保安検査
hoan kensa

passport control
出入国審査
shutsunyūkoku shinsa

gate
ゲート
gēto

e-ticket
Eチケット
ii chiketto

| | | |
|---|---|---|
| customs<br>税関<br>zēkan | seatbelt<br>シートベルト<br>shiitoberuto | hand luggage<br>機内持ち込み手荷物<br>kinai mochikomi tenimotsu |
| cabin crew<br>乗務員<br>jōmuin | engine<br>エンジン<br>enjin | cabin baggage<br>機内持ち込み荷物<br>kinai mochikomi nimotsu |
| business class<br>ビジネスクラス<br>bijinesu kurasu | wings<br>翼<br>tsubasa | connecting flight<br>乗り継ぎ便<br>noritsugi bin |
| economy class<br>エコノミークラス<br>ekonomii kurasu | fuselage<br>機体<br>kitai | jetlag<br>時差ぼけ<br>jisaboke |
| aisle<br>通路<br>tsūro | hold<br>貨物室<br>kamotsushitsu | to check in<br>搭乗手続きをする<br>tōjōtetsuzuki o suru |
| overhead locker<br>天井収納庫<br>tenjōshūnōko | hold luggage<br>手荷物の預け入れ<br>tenimotsu no azukeire | to check in online<br>オンラインチェックインをする<br>onrain chekkuin o suru |
| tray table<br>テーブル<br>tēburu | excess baggage<br>超過手荷物<br>chōka tenimotsu | |

aeroplane
飛行機
hikōki

airport
空港
kūkō

baggage reclaim
手荷物受取
tenimotsu uketori

boarding card
搭乗券
tōjōken

cabin
客室
kyakushitsu

check-in desk
搭乗手続きカウンター
tōjō tetsuzuki kauntā

cockpit
コックピット
kokkupitto

departure board
出発掲示板
shuppatsu kējiban

duty-free shop
免税店
menzēten

holdall
大型手提げかばん
ōgata tesage kaban

luggage trolley
手荷物カート
tenimotsu kāto

passport
パスポート
pasupōto

pilot
パイロット
pairotto

runway
滑走路
kassōro

suitcase
スーツケース
sūtsukēsu

Long-distance ferries still link the four main islands, while local ferries serve hundreds of smaller islands.

### YOU MIGHT SAY…

When is the next boat to…?
次の…行きの船はいつですか。
tsugi no …iki no fune wa itsu desu ka?

Where does the boat leave from?
船はどこから出ますか。
fune wa doko kara demasu ka?

What time is the last boat to…?
…行きの最後の船は何時ですか。
…iki no saigo no fune wa nan-ji desu ka?

How long is the trip/crossing?
乗船時間はどれぐらいですか。
jōsen jikan wa dore gurai desu ka?

How many crossings a day are there?
1日に船は何便ありますか。
ichinichi ni fune wa nan-bin arimasu ka?

How much for … passengers?
…人はいくらですか。
…nin wa ikura desu ka?

How much is it for a vehicle?
車の予約はいくらですか。
kuruma no yoyaku wa ikura desu ka?

I feel seasick.
船酔いしました。
funayoi shimashita.

### YOU MIGHT HEAR…

The boat leaves from…
船は…から出ます。
fune wa … kara demasu.

The trip/crossing lasts…
乗船時間は…です。
jōsen jikan wa … desu.

There are … crossings a day.
1日に…便あります。
ichinichi ni …bin arimasu.

The ferry is delayed/cancelled.
フェリーは遅れています／キャンセルになりました。
ferii wa okurete imasu/kyanseru ni narimashita.

Sea conditions are good/bad.
海は穏やかです／荒れています。
umi wa odayaka desu/arete imasu.

ferry terminal
フェリーターミナル
ferii tāminaru

port
港
minato

foot passenger
通行人
tsūkōnin

lifeboat
救命ボート
kyūmē bōto

pier
桟橋
sanbashi

to board
乗船する
jōsen suru

deck
デッキ
dekki

captain
キャプテン
kyaputen

to leave port
出航する
shukkō suru

car deck
車両甲板
sharyō kanpan

crew
乗組員
norikumi-in

to dock
埠頭につく
futō ni tsuku

**GENERAL**

anchor
アンカー
ankā

buoy
ブイ
bui

canal
運河
unga

gangway
タラップ
tarappu

harbour
入り江
irie

jetty
桟橋
sanbashi

lifebuoy
救命ブイ
kyūmēbui

lifejacket
救命胴衣
kyūmēdōi

mooring
係船
kēsen

**BOATS**

canoe
カヌー
kanū

coastguard boat
沿岸警備隊ボート
engan-kēbitai bōto

ferry
フェリー
ferii

inflatable dinghy
インフレータブル・
ミニボート
infurētaburu minibōto

kayak
カヤック
kayakku

liner
大型定期船
ōgata tēkisen

rowing boat
（オールでこぐ）ボート
(ōru de kogu) bōto

sailing boat
ヨット
yotto

yacht
ヨット
yotto

50

## IN THE HOME | 家で

Japan is attracting an increasing number of tourists and expats who are looking for a place to call home for a time, whether it is a short-term let in a studio apartment for one, or communal living in a hostel or guest house.

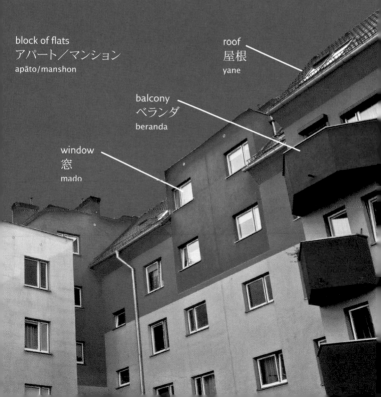

block of flats
アパート／マンション
apāto/manshon

roof
屋根
yane

balcony
ベランダ
beranda

window
窓
mado

Many Japanese in cities live in flats (アパート apāto) and the better-quality ones are called マンション (manshon - from English "mansion" but very different!). Detached houses are found in the suburbs and towns.

### YOU MIGHT SAY...

I live in...
…に住んでいます。
...ni sunde imasu.

I'm staying at...
…に泊まっています。
...ni tomatte imasu.

My address is...
住所は…です。
jūsho wa ...desu.

I'm the homeowner/tenant.
持ち家／借家です。
mochi-ie/shakuya desu.

I like this area.
この地域が好きですです。
kono chiiki ga suki desu.

I'd like to buy/rent a property here.
ここの家を買いたい／借りたいんですが。
koko no ie o kaitai/karitai n desu ga.

### YOU MIGHT HEAR...

Where do you live?
どこに住んでいますか。
doko ni sunde imasu ka?

Where are you staying?
どこに泊まっていますか。
doko ni tomatte imasu ka?

What's your address, please?
ご住所をお願いします。
go-jūsho o onegai shimasu.

Are you the owner/tenant?
持ち家／借家ですか。
mochi-ie/shakuya desu ka?

### VOCABULARY

bungalow
平屋建て
hiraya-date

building
建物
tatemono

address
住所
jūsho

suburb
郊外
kōgai

district
街／地区
machi/chiku

letting/estate agent
不動産屋
fudōsan-ya

| | | |
|---|---|---|
| landlord/landlady<br>家主<br>yanushi | rent<br>家賃<br>yachin | to own<br>持っている<br>motte iru |
| tenant<br>借家人<br>shakuyanin | rental agreement<br>賃貸借契約<br>chintaishaku kēyaku | to live<br>住んでいる<br>sunde iru |
| mortgage<br>住宅ローン<br>jūtaku-rōn | to rent<br>借りる<br>kariru | to move house<br>引っ越す<br>hikkosu |

## YOU SHOULD KNOW...

Cities and towns are generally divided into blocks rather than streets. Name plates are used to identify houses and letterboxes within apartments; some may have Romanized versions as well as the usual Japanese script.

## TYPES OF BUILDING

apartment block
アパート／マンション
apāto/manshon

detached house
一戸建て
ikko-date

farmhouse
農家
nōka

hotel
ホテル
hoteru

inn
旅館
ryokan

public housing complex
団地
danchi

# THE HOUSE | 家

Housing is described in terms of rooms plus kitchen/diner, so a 2DK has two rooms plus kitchen/diner, bathroom and toilet.

## YOU MIGHT SAY...

There's a problem with...
…に問題があります。
…ni mondai ga arimasu.

We have a power cut.
停電しました。
tēden shimashita.

It's not working.
駄目になっています。
dame ni natte imasu.

Can you recommend anyone?
誰か紹介してくれませんか。
dareka shōkai shite kuremasen ka?

The drains are blocked.
配水管が詰まりました。
haisuikan ga tsumarimashita.

Can it be repaired?
直りますか。
naorimasu ka?

The boiler has broken.
ボイラーが故障しました。
boirā ga koshō shimashita.

I can smell gas/smoke.
ガス／煙のにおいがします。
gasu/kemuri no nioi ga shimasu.

There's no hot water.
お湯が出ません。
o-yu ga demasen.

We have a water leak.
水が漏れています。
mizu ga morete imasu.

## YOU MIGHT HEAR...

What seems to be the problem?
どんな問題のようですか。
donna mondai no yō desu ka?

Where is the meter/fusebox?
メーター／ヒューズボックスはどこですか。
mētā/hyūzu-bokkusu wa doko desu ka?

## YOU SHOULD KNOW...

As construction methods are different in Japan, it is best to ask a Japanese person to contact an appropriate company to send out a repair person (修理屋 shūriya), if any problems arise.

| room<br>部屋<br>heya | shutter<br>窓シャッター<br>mado shattā | adaptor<br>ソケットアダプタ<br>soketto adaputa |
|---|---|---|
| floor<br>床<br>yuka | aerial<br>アンテナ<br>antena | socket<br>コンセント<br>konsento |
| ceiling<br>天井<br>tenjō | satellite dish<br>衛星放送用アンテナ<br>ēsē hōsōyō antena | electricity<br>電気<br>denki |
| wall<br>壁<br>kabe | air conditioning<br>空調<br>kūchō | gas<br>ガス<br>gasu |
| back door<br>裏口<br>uraguchi | battery<br>乾電池<br>kandenchi | repair<br>修理<br>shūri |
| sliding door<br>雨戸<br>amado | electric cable<br>コード<br>kōdo | to fix<br>修理する<br>shūri suru |
| skylight<br>天窓<br>tenmado | plug<br>プラグ<br>puragu | to ask for an estimate<br>見積もりを頼む<br>mitsumori o tanomu |

## INSIDE

boiler
ボイラー
boirā

extension cable
延長コード
enchōkōdo

fusebox
ヒューズボックス
hyūzubokkusu

**heater**
ヒーター
hiitā

**light bulb**
電球
denkyū

**meter**
メーター
mētā

**security alarm**
防犯警報装置
bōhan kēhōsōchi

**smoke alarm**
煙感知器
kemuri-kanchiki

**thermostat**
サーモスタット
sāmosutatto

### OUTSIDE

| | | | |
|---|---|---|---|
| roof | gutter | drainpipe | window |
| 屋根 | とい | 排水管 | 窓 |
| yane | toi | haisuikan | mado |

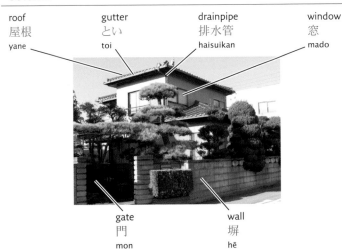

gate
門
mon

wall
塀
hē

Front doors open outwards, so if you are visiting someone's house, stand back! Traditional houses and Japanese inns may have sliding doors; at the latter, it is polite to slide the door open a little and call out ごめんください！ (gomen kudasai!). All houses and flats have an entrance area called the 玄関 (genkan). It is here that you always take off and leave your shoes and then step up onto the main floor of the house, where slippers are used (provided for guests).

## YOU MIGHT SAY/HEAR...

Would you like to come round?
うちにいらっしゃいませんか。
uchi ni irasshaimasen ka?

Make yourself at home.
お楽になさってください。
o-raku ni nasatte kudasai.

Hello. Please come in.
どうぞ、お上がりください。
dōzo o-agari kudasai.

This is a little something for you.
つまらないものですが。
tsumaranai mono desu ga.

Shall I take your coat?
コートをお預かりしましょうか。
kōto o o-azukari shimashō ka?

Can I use your bathroom?
トイレをお借りしてもいいですか。
toire o o-kari shite mo ii desu ka?

Here are some slippers.
スリッパをどうぞ。
suripa o dōzo.

Thanks for inviting me over.
お招きいただいて、ありがとうございます。
o-maneki itadaite arigatō gozaimasu.

## YOU SHOULD KNOW...

Visitors should apologize for intruding when they step up into the house:
お邪魔します (o-jama shimasu).

## VOCABULARY

| front door | doormat | key |
|---|---|---|
| 玄関ドア | 玄関マット | 鍵 |
| genkan doa | genkan-matto | kagi |

| | | |
|---|---|---|
| letterbox<br>郵便受け<br>yūbin-uke | staircase<br>階段<br>kaidan | to ring the bell/press the buzzer<br>ベル／ブザーを押す<br>beru/buzā o osu |
| corridor<br>廊下<br>rōka | landing<br>踊り場<br>odoriba | to let somebody in<br>（人）を入れる<br>(hito) o ireru |
| hallway<br>玄関<br>genkan | banister<br>手すり<br>tesuri | to take off one's shoes<br>靴を脱ぐ<br>kutsu o nugu |

doorbell
呼び鈴
yobirin

intercom
インターホーン
intāhōn

lift
エレベーター
erebētā

peephole
ドアスコープ
doa-sukōpu

shoe cupboard
靴箱／下駄箱
kutsubako/getabako

slippers
スリッパ
surippa

A traditional Japanese room is a flexible living space, used as lounge, dining room, study, and bedroom. The flooring is tatami matting. In the daytime, a low table is used for eating and studying, and people kneel or sit on flat floor cushions or legless chairs. At night, the table is put away to the side of the room, and the futon mattresses and quilts laid out. All the family sleep side by side in the same room. In winter, a special low table with a heating element underneath こたつ (kotatsu) is used.

floor cushion
座布団
zabuton

futon
布団
futon

hanging scroll
掛け軸
kakejiku

heated table
こたつ
kotatsu

Japanese veranda
縁側
engawa

legless chair
座椅子
zaisu

low table
座卓
zataku

paper wall panel
障子
shōji

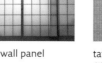

tatami matting
畳
tatami

## VOCABULARY

carpet
カーペット
kaapetto

picture
絵
e

ceiling light
蛍光灯
kēkōtō

rug
じゅうたん
jūtan

ornament
装飾品
sōshokuhin

to relax
くつろぐ
kutsurogu

sofa bed
ソファーベッド
sofābeddo

lampshade
電気のかさ
denki no kasa

to watch TV
テレビをみる
terebi o miru

## GENERAL

blind
ブラインド
buraindo

curtains
カーテン
kāten

DVD/Blu-ray® player
DVD／ブルーレイ
プレイヤー
dii-bui-dii/brūrē purēyā

electric fan
扇風機
senpūki

radio
ラジオ
rajio

remote control
リモコン
rimokon

table lamp
電気スタンド
denki-sutando

TV
テレビ
terebi

TV stand
テレビ台
terebi-dai

## LOUNGE

floor
床
yuka

bookcase
本棚
hondana

sofa
ソファー
sofā

cushion
クッション
kusshon

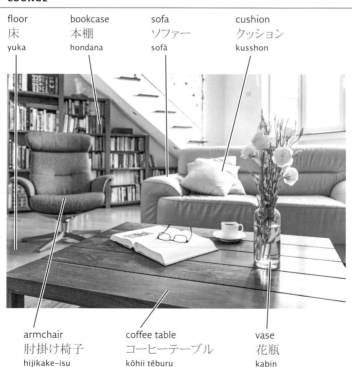

armchair
肘掛け椅子
hijikake-isu

coffee table
コーヒーテーブル
kōhii tēburu

vase
花瓶
kabin

Small ovens and dishwashers are recent additions to Japanese kitchens but are by no means ubiquitous, and most Japanese cooking is still done on the hob. Electric rice cookers make that particular cooking task easy, and instead of electric kettles, there are electric instant hot water pots.

### VOCABULARY

to cook
料理する
ryōri suru

to wash up
皿を洗う
sara o arau

to clean the worktops
調理台をきれいに
する
chōridai o kirē ni suru

to put away the groceries
食料をしまう
shokuryō o shimau

### MISCELLANEOUS ITEMS

aluminium foil
アルミ箔
arumihaku

bin bag
ゴミ袋
gomibukuro

clingfilm
ラップ
rappu

kitchen roll
ペーパータオル
pēpā taoru

pedal bin
ペダルビン
pedaru-bin

washing-up sponge
スポンジ
suponji

baking tray
天パン
tenpan

cafetière
コーヒープレス
kōhii-puresu

chopping board
まな板
manaita

colander
水きりボウル
mizukiri-bouru

corkscrew
コルク抜き
koruku-nuki

fish slice
フライ返し
furaigaeshi

food processor
フードプロセッサー
fūdo-purosessā

frying pan
フライパン
furaipan

grater
おろし器
oroshiki

hand mixer
ハンドミキサー
hando-mikisā

kettle
やかん
yakan

kitchen knife
包丁
hōchō

ladle
おたま
otama

measuring jug
計量カップ
kēryō-kappu

mixing bowl
ボウル
bouru

peeler
皮むき器
kawamukiki

rice cooker
炊飯器
suihanki

rolling pin
めん棒
menbō

saucepan
鍋
nabe

sieve
ざる
zaru

spatula
へら
hera

teapot
ティーポット
tiipotto

tin opener
缶切り
kankiri

toaster oven
オーブントースター
ōbun-tōsutā

whisk
泡だて器
awadateki

wok
中華鍋
chūka-nabe

wooden spoon
木のスプーン
ki no supūn

**THE KITCHEN**

sink
シンク
shinku

oven
オーブン
ōbun

hob
コンロ
konro

microwave
電子レンジ
denshi-renji

fridge-freezer
冷凍冷蔵庫
rētōrēzōko

tap
蛇口
jaguchi

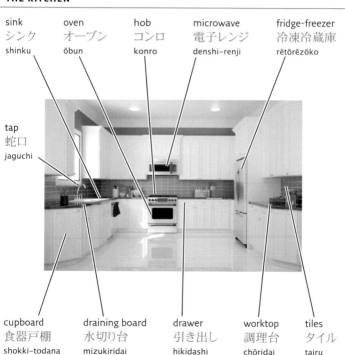

cupboard
食器戸棚
shokki-todana

draining board
水切り台
mizukiridai

drawer
引き出し
hikidashi

worktop
調理台
chōridai

tiles
タイル
tairu

The kitchen and dining area are generally combined in Japanese homes. People may invite close friends to their homes for a meal, but otherwise they generally prefer to invite people out to a restaurant.

## VOCABULARY

| | | |
|---|---|---|
| dining table<br>食卓<br>shokutaku | coaster<br>コースター<br>kōsutā | to set the table<br>食卓の準備をする<br>shokutaku no junbi o suru |
| chair<br>椅子<br>isu | crockery<br>陶器<br>tōki | to dine<br>食事をする<br>shokuji o suru |
| place mat<br>ランチョンマット<br>ranchon matto | glassware<br>ガラス食器<br>garasu shokki | to clear the table<br>食卓を片付ける<br>shokutaku o katazukeru |

chopsticks
箸
hashi

chopstick rest
箸置き
hashi-oki

cup and saucer
カップと受け皿
kappu to ukezara

Japanese teapot
きゅうす
kyūsu

knife and fork
ナイフとフォーク
naifu to fōku

miso soup bowl
おわん
o-wan

napkin
ナプキン
napukin

plate
皿
sara

rice bowl
茶碗
chawan

sake cup
おちょこ
o-choko

sake flask
とっくり
tokkuri

salad bowl
サラダボウル
sarada bouru

spoon
スプーン
supūn

tea cup
湯呑茶碗
yunomijawan

teaspoon
ティースプーン
tii-supūn

tumbler
タンブラー
tanburā

water jug
水差し
mizusashi

wine glass
ワイングラス
wain-gurasu

### VOCABULARY

| | | |
|---|---|---|
| single bed<br>シングルベッド<br>shinguru beddo | to go to bed<br>寝る<br>neru | to make the bed<br>ベッドの準備をする<br>beddo no junbi o suru |
| double bed<br>ダブルベッド<br>daburu beddo | to sleep<br>眠る<br>nemuru | to change the sheets<br>シーツを替える<br>shiitsu o kaeru |
| spare room<br>予備の寝室<br>yobi no shinshitsu | to wake up<br>目が覚める<br>me ga sameru | to air the futon<br>布団を干す<br>futon o hosu |

### GENERAL

alarm clock
目覚まし時計
mezamashi dokei

bedding
寝具
shingu

blanket
毛布
mōfu

bunk beds
二段ベッド
nidan-beddo

coat hanger
ハンガー
hangā

dressing table
鏡台／ドレッサー
kyōdai/doressā

hairdryer
ドライヤー
doraiyā

laundry basket
洗濯かご
sentaku-kago

sheets
シーツ
shiitsu

**BEDROOM**

mirror
鏡
kagami

chest of drawers
タンス
tansu

bed
ベッド
beddo

duvet
掛け布団
kakebuton

wardrobe
衣装ダンス
ishōdansu

curtains
カーテン
kāten

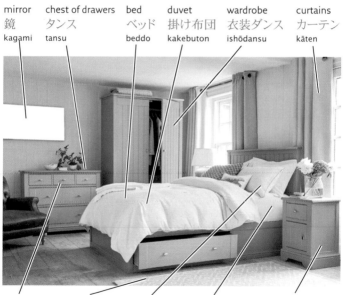

drawer
引き出し
hikidashi

rug
じゅうたん
jūtan

pillow
枕
makura

mattress
マットレス
mattoresu

bedside table
ベッドサイドテーブル
beddosaido tēburu

Traditionally, the toilet was separate from the bathroom but in modern small apartments, the space-saving all-in-one bathroom module (ユニットバス yunitto basu) is replacing the separate rooms.

## VOCABULARY

| | | |
|---|---|---|
| sink<br>シンク<br>shinku | to have a shower/bath<br>シャワーを浴びる/<br>お風呂に入る<br>shawā o abiru/<br>o-furo ni hairu | to brush one's teeth<br>歯を磨く<br>ha o migaku |
| toilet<br>トイレ<br>toire | to wash one's hands<br>手を洗う<br>te o arau | to go to the toilet<br>トイレに行く<br>toire ni iku |

## GENERAL

Japanese towel
手ぬぐい
tenugui

toilet roll
トイレットペーパー
toiretto pēpā

towel
タオル
taoru

## BATHROOM

tap
蛇口
jaguchi

shower
シャワー
shawā

bath
浴槽
yokusō

mirror
鏡
kagami

Japanese gardens are famous for their aesthetics of restraint and calm, featuring water, gravel, trees, and moss. Domestic gardens tend to be similar, although gardens with lawns and flower beds are becoming more popular.

### VOCABULARY

| | | |
|---|---|---|
| tree<br>木<br>ki | moss<br>苔<br>koke | gardener<br>庭師<br>niwashi |
| soil<br>土<br>tsuchi | gravel<br>小石<br>koishi | to weed<br>雑草を取る<br>zassō o toru |
| grass<br>草<br>kusa | bonsai<br>盆栽<br>bonsai | to water<br>水をかける<br>mizu o kakeru |
| plant<br>植物<br>shokubutsu | compost<br>堆肥<br>taihi | to grow<br>育てる<br>sodateru |
| weed<br>雑草<br>zassō | allotment<br>市民農園<br>shimin nōen | to plant<br>植える<br>ueru |

### GARDEN

path<br>小道<br>komichi

lawn<br>芝生<br>shibafu

flowerbed<br>花壇<br>kadan

fence<br>塀<br>hē

flowers<br>花<br>hana

flowerpot<br>植木鉢<br>uekibachi

**bonsai scissors**
盆栽ばさみ
bonsai-basami

**garden fork**
熊手
kumade

**gardening gloves**
ガーデニング用手袋
gādeningu-yō tebukuro

**garden hose**
ホース
hōsu

**lawnmower**
芝刈り機
shibakariki

**pruners**
はさみ
hasami

**rake**
熊手
kumade

**spade**
シャベル
shaberu

**trowel**
移植ごて
ishokugote

**watering can**
じょうろ
jōro

**weedkiller**
除草剤
josōzai

**wheelbarrow**
手押し車
teoshiguruma

## VOCABULARY

household appliances
家庭用設備
katē-yō setsubi

dishwasher tablet
食洗器用洗剤
shokusenki-yō senzai

to do the laundry
洗濯する
sentaku suru

chores
毎日の雑用
mainichi no zatsuyō

laundry detergent
洗剤
senzai

to hoover
掃除機をかける
sōjiki o kakeru

bleach
漂白剤
hyōhakuzai

washing-up liquid
食器洗い洗剤
shokkiarai senzai

to tidy up
片付ける
katazukeru

disinfectant
消毒液
shōdoku-eki

to sweep the floor
床をはく
yuka o haku

to clean
掃除する
sōji suru

brush
ブラシ
burashi

bucket
バケツ
baketsu

cloth
雑巾
zōkin

clothes horse
物干し
monohoshi

clothes pegs
洗濯ばさみ
sentaku-basami

dishwasher
食洗器
shokusenki

dustbin
ゴミ箱
gomibako

dustpan
ちり取り
chiritori

iron
アイロン
airon

ironing board
アイロン台
airon-dai

laundry pole
物干しざお
monohoshi-zao

mop
モップ
moppu

rubber gloves
ゴム手袋
gomu-tebukuro

scourer
ナイロンたわし
nairon-tawashi

tumble drier
乾燥機
kansōki

vacuum cleaner
掃除機
sōjiki

washing machine
洗濯機
sentakuki

wastepaper basket
ゴミ箱
gomibako

# AT THE SHOPS | 店で

Shopping is a popular leisure activity in Japan. Excellent customer service is highly valued, whether in high-class department stores selling luxury goods, or in small shops.

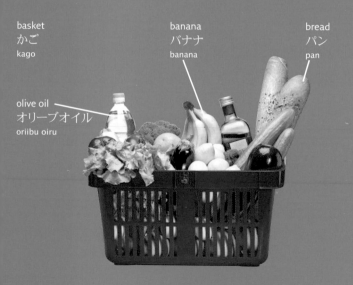

**basket**
かご
kago

**banana**
バナナ
banana

**bread**
パン
pan

**olive oil**
オリーブオイル
oriibu oiru

From traditional craft products to the most up-to-date technology and fashion, Japan has something for every taste. Many shops open later than in the UK, generally at 10 a.m., but are then open until 8 p.m. or later, while convenience stores are open 24 hours a day. Sunday is a very popular shopping day.

**YOU MIGHT SAY...**

Where is the...?
…はどこですか。
...wa doko desu ka?

Where is the nearest...?
一番近い…はどこですか。
ichiban chikai ...wa doko desu ka?

Where can I buy...?
…はどこで買えますか。
...wa doko de kaemasu ka?

What time do you open/close?
何時に開きます／閉まりますか。
nan-ji ni akimasu/shimarimasu ka?

I'm just looking, thanks.
見ているだけです。
mite iru dake desu.

Do you sell...?
…を売っていますか。
...o utte imasu ka?

May I have...?
…をください。
...o kudasai.

Can I pay by card?
カードで払えますか。
kādo de haraemasu ka?

How much does this cost?
これはいくらですか。
kore wa ikura desu ka?

How much is delivery?
配達はいくらかかりますか。
haitatsu wa ikura kakarimasu ka?

I would like...
…がほしいんですが。
...ga hoshii n desu ga.

Can I exchange this?
これを交換してもらえますか。
kore o kōkan shite moraemasu ka?

Can I get a refund?
払い戻してもらえますか。
haraimodoshite moraemasu ka?

That's all, thank you.
それだけです。ありがとう。
sore dake desu. arigatō.

Welcome. Can I help you?
いらっしゃいませ。
irasshaimase.

How would you like to pay?
お支払方法は？
o-shiharai hōhō wa?

Would you like anything else?
他に何かございますか。
hoka ni nanika gozaimasu ka?

Can you enter your PIN?
暗証番号をお願いします。
anshō-bangō o onegai shimasu.

It costs...
…円でございます。
...en de gozaimasu.

Would you like a receipt?
領収書／レシートは要りますか。
ryōshūsho/reshiito wa irimasu ka?

Shall I order that for you?
注文いたしましょうか。
chūmon itashimashō ka?

Have you got a receipt?
レシートをお持ちですか。
reshiito o o-mochi desu ka?

## VOCABULARY

shop
店
mise

shopping centre
ショッピングセンター
shoppingu sentā

PIN
暗証番号
anshōbangō

shop assistant
店員
ten'in

market
市場
ichiba

discount voucher/
coupon
割引券
waribiki-ken

customer
お客さん／様
o-kyaku-san/-sama

groceries
食料品
shokuryōhin

gift card/voucher
ギフトカード／ギフト券
gifuto-kādo/gifuto-ken

convenience store
コンビニ
konbini

cash
現金
genkin

exchange
交換
kōkan

supermarket
スーパー
sūpā

change
おつり
o-tsuri

refund
払い戻し
haraimodoshi

77

**return**
返品
henpin

**to pay**
払う
harau

**to do the shopping/
go shopping**
買いものをする／
に行く
kaimono o suru/ni iku

**contactless**
コンタクトレス
kontakutoresu

**to shop online**
オンラインで買い物
をする
onrain de kaimono o
suru

**to browse**
あれこれ見て回る
are kore mite mawaru

**to buy**
買う
kau

**banknotes**
紙幣
shihē

**card reader**
カード読取り機
kādo yomitoriki

**coins**
硬貨
kōka

**debit/credit card**
デビット／クレジッ
トカード
debitto/kurejitto kādo

**plastic bag**
レジ袋
reji-bukuro

**receipt**
レシート
reshiito

**shopping district**
商店街
shōtengai

**till point**
（お）会計
(o)kaikē

**wrapping paper**
包装紙
hōsōshi

Supermarkets are usually open from 10 a.m. to around 10 p.m. and convenience stores are open 24 hours a day. Carrier bags are usually provided, although there is often a small charge. Convenience stores sell a range of ready-made food and essentials, including postage stamps. They also offer many services, including photocopying, parcel dispatch and collection, bill payments, ticket sales, and ATMs.

### YOU MIGHT SAY...

Where can I find...?
…はどこにありますか。
...wa doko ni arimasu ka?

I'm looking for...
…を探しています。
...o sagashite imasu.

I don't need a carrier bag.
レジ袋は要りません。
reji-bukuro wa irimasen.

### YOU MIGHT HEAR...

It's in the ... section.
…売り場にございます。
...uriba ni gozaimasu.

Shall I help you pack your bags?
お詰めしましょうか。
o-tsume shimashō ka?

There is a charge for a carrier bag.
レジ袋は有料です。
reji-bukuro wa yūryō desu.

### VOCABULARY

| | | |
|---|---|---|
| aisle<br>通路<br>tsūro | jar<br>ジャー<br>jā | frozen<br>冷凍<br>rētō |
| bottle<br>ビン<br>bin | packet<br>袋<br>fukuro | dairy<br>乳製品<br>nyūsēhin |
| box<br>箱<br>hako | tin<br>缶<br>kan | low-fat<br>低脂肪<br>tēshibō |
| carton<br>カートン<br>kāton | fresh<br>新鮮な<br>shinsen-na | low-calorie<br>低カロリー<br>tēkarorii |

**basket**
かご
kago

**scales**
はかり
hakari

**trolley**
ショッピングカート
shoppingu kāto

## JAPANESE FOODS

**bean curd**
豆腐
tōfu

**brown rice**
玄米
genmai

**buckwheat noodles**
そば
soba

**Chinese noodles**
ラーメン
rāmen

**dried bonito flakes**
鰹節
katsuoboshi

**fermented soy beans**
納豆
nattō

**hijiki seaweed**
ひじき
hijiki

**Japanese fishcake**
かまぼこ
kamaboko

**Japanese stock**
だし
dashi

kelp
昆布
konbu

nori seaweed sheets
海苔
nori

pickled plums
梅干し
umeboshi

pickled vegetables
漬物
tsukemono

(red/white/mixed) soy bean paste
(赤／白／合わせ)味噌
(aka/shiro/awase) miso

rice
米
kome

soy sauce
醤油
shōyu

sweetened rice wine
味醂
mirin

vinegar/rice vinegar
酢／米酢
su/komezu

wakame seaweed
ワカメ
wakame

wasabi
わさび
wasabi

wheat noodles
うどん
udon

herbs
ハーブ
hābu

honey
ハチミツ
hachimitsu

jam
ジャム
jamu

ketchup
ケチャップ
ketchappu

mayonnaise
マヨネーズ
mayonēzu

mustard
辛子
karashi

olive oil
オリーブオイル
oriibu oiru

pasta
パスタ
pasuta

pepper
こしょう
koshō

salt
塩
shio

spices
スパイス
supaisu

sugar
砂糖
satō

chocolate
チョコレート
chokorēto

crisps
ポテトチップス
poteto-chippusu

ice cream
アイスクリーム
aisukuriimu

Japanese dumpling
団子
dango

Japanese stuffed pancake
どら焼き
dorayaki

nuts
ナッツ
nattsu

popcorn
ポップコーン
poppukōn

rice crackers
せんべい
senbē

sweets
菓子
kashi

barley tea
麦茶
mugicha

beer
ビール
biiru

(black) tea
紅茶
kōcha

brown rice green tea
玄米茶
genmaicha

fizzy drink
炭酸ドリンク
tansan dorinku

fruit juice
フルーツジュース
furūtsu-jūsu

green tea
お茶／煎茶
o-cha/sencha

ground coffee
挽いたコーヒー
hiita kōhii

iced coffee
アイスコーヒー
aisu kōhii

instant coffee
インスタントコーヒー
insutanto kōhii

mineral water
ミネラルウォーター
mineraru wōtā

roasted green tea
ほうじ茶
hōjicha

sake
酒／日本酒
sake/nihonshu

spirits
蒸留酒
jōryūshu

wine
ワイン
wain

Tsukiji fish market in Tokyo is famous, but there are plenty of other markets selling seafood, fresh produce, and other food. You will also find antique and flea markets in parks and temple grounds. Some markets are open most days, others weekly or monthly.

## YOU MIGHT SAY...

Where is the market?
市場はどこですか。
ichiba wa doko desu ka?

When is market day?
市場は何日ですか。
ichiba wa nan-nichi desu ka?

100 grams/A kilo of...
…を100グラム／一キロ。
...o hyaku-guramu/ichi kiro.

A slice of ..., please.
…を一切れ、ください。
...o hito-kire kudasai.

## YOU MIGHT HEAR...

The market is in that building over there.
市場はあの建物の中です。
ichiba wa ano tatemono no naka desu.

What would you like?
何を差し上げましょうか。
nani o sashiagemashō ka?

Here you are. Anything else?
どうぞ。他に何かありますか。
dōzo. hoka ni nanika arimasu ka?

Here's your change.
おつりです。
o-tsuri desu.

## VOCABULARY

| | | |
|---|---|---|
| marketplace 市場 ichiba | customers お客さん o-kyaku-san | organic 有機栽培の yūkisaibai no |
| flea market フリーマーケット furii-māketto | stall 屋台店 yataimise | seasonal 旬の shun no |
| produce 作物 sakumotsu | local 地元の jimoto no | home-made 自家製 jikasē |

## VOCABULARY

| | | |
|---|---|---|
| greengrocer<br>八百屋<br>yaoya | seed/pip/stone<br>種<br>tane | fresh<br>新鮮な<br>shinsen-na |
| juice<br>ジュース<br>jūsu | skin<br>皮<br>kawa | rotten<br>腐った<br>kusatta |
| leaf<br>葉<br>ha | seedless<br>種なし<br>tane-nashi | ripe<br>熟した<br>jukushita |
| rind/peel<br>皮<br>kawa | raw<br>生<br>nama | unripe<br>熟していない<br>jukushite inai |

## FRUIT

apple
リンゴ
ringo

avocado
アボカド
abokado

banana
バナナ
banana

blueberry
ブルーベリー
burūberii

cherry
チェリー
cherii

chestnut
栗
kuri

fig
いちじく
ichijiku

grape
ブドウ
budō

grapefruit
グレープフルーツ
gurēpufurūtsu

Japanese pear
梨
nashi

kiwi fruit
キーウィ
kiiwi

lemon
レモン
remon

loquat
びわ
biwa

mango
マンゴ
mango

melon
メロン
meron

navel orange
ネーブル
nēburu

nectarine
ネクタリン
nekutarin

orange
オレンジ
orenji

papaya
パパイヤ
papaiya

peach
モモ
momo

persimmon
柿
kaki

pineapple
パイナップル
painappuru

plum
スモモ
sumomo

pomegranate
ザクロ
zakuro

redcurrant
赤スグリ
aka suguri

satsuma
みかん
mikan

strawberry
イチゴ
ichigo

ume plum
梅
ume

watermelon
スイカ
suika

yuzu
ゆず
yuzu

asparagus
アスパラガス
asuparagasu

aubergine
ナス
nasu

bamboo shoots
タケノコ
takenoko

broccoli
ブロッコリー
burokkorii

cabbage
キャベツ
kyabetsu

carrot
ニンジン
ninjin

cauliflower
カリフラワー
karifurawā

celery
セロリ
serori

chilli
トウガラシ
tōgarashi

Chinese cabbage
白菜
hakusai

courgette
ズッキーニ
zukkiini

cucumber
きゅうり
kyūri

garlic
ニンニク
ninniku

ginger
ショウガ
shōga

green beans
さやいんげん
sayaingen

Japanese mushrooms
キノコ
kinoko

leek
リーキー
riikii

lettuce
レタス
retasu

lotus root
レンコン
renkon

mooli
大根
daikon

mushrooms
マッシュルーム
masshurūmu

onion
タマネギ
tamanegi

pak choi
チンゲン菜
chingensai

peas
グリーンピース
guriinpiisu

potato
ジャガイモ
jagaimo

red pepper
赤いピーマン
akai piiman

shiitake mushrooms
しいたけ
shiitake

shiso
しそ
shiso

spinach
ほうれん草
hōrensō

spring onion
ネギ
negi

sweetcorn
トウモロコシ
tōmorokoshi

sweet potato
サツマイモ
satsumaimo

tomato
トマト
tomato

Although some European-style wholemeal bread is available in department stores or specialized bakeries, the soft white 食パン (shoku-pan) loaf, often thickly sliced, is ubiquitous. Sweet or savoury filled rolls 菓子パン (kashi-pan) are also common, as are steamed buns filled with meat, 肉まん (nikuman), or azuki bean paste, あんまん (an-pan).

### YOU MIGHT SAY...

May I have...?
…をください。
...o kudasai.

Two/three ..., please.
…をふたつ／みっつ、ください。
...o futatsu/mittsu, kudasai.

### YOU MIGHT HEAR...

Would you like anything else?
他に何かございますか。
hoka ni nanika gozaimasu ka?

I'm sorry, we don't have...
申し訳ありません。…はございません。
mōshiwake arimasen. ...wa gozaimasen.

### VOCABULARY

baker
パン屋
pan-ya

bread
パン
pan

wholemeal bread
全粒粉パン
zenryūfun-pan

flour
小麦粉
komugiko

gluten-free
グルテンが入っていない
guruten ga haitte inai

to bake
焼く
yaku

adzuki bean bun
アンパン
an-pan

baguette
フランスパン
furansu-pan

bread rolls
ロールパン
rōru-pan

brioche
ブリオッシュ
buriosshu

croissant
クロワッサン
kurowassan

curry bun
カレーパン
karē-pan

Danish pastry
デニッシュペストリー
denisshu pēsutorii

doughnut
ドーナツ
dōnatsu

éclair
エクレア
ekurea

pancakes
ホットケーキ
hottokēki

sliced loaf
食パン
shoku-pan

sweet/savoury bun
菓子パン
kashi-pan

Butcher's shops (and other individual stores) are becoming increasingly scarce in Japan, but they still exist in towns, including some halal butchers in Tokyo. Of course, there are also meat counters in department stores and supermarkets.

### YOU MIGHT SAY...

A kilo of...
…を1キロ
...o ichi-kiro

A slice of..., please.
…を一切れ、ください。
...o hito-kire kudasai.

Can you slice this for me, please?
薄切りにしてもらえますか。
usugiri ni shite moraemasu ka?

### YOU MIGHT HEAR...

Certainly, sir/madam.
分かりました。
wakarimashita.

How much would you like?
どのぐらい差し上げましょうか。
dono gurai sashiagemashō ka?

How many would you like?
いくつ差し上げましょうか。
ikutsu sashiagemashō ka?

### VOCABULARY

| | | |
|---|---|---|
| butcher<br>肉屋<br>niku-ya | cold meats<br>冷肉<br>rēniku | mutton<br>マトン<br>maton |
| meat<br>肉<br>niku | sliced meat<br>薄切り肉<br>usugiri niku | pork<br>豚肉／ポーク<br>butaniku/pōku |
| red meat<br>赤身の肉<br>akami no niku | beef<br>牛肉／ビーフ<br>gyūniku/biifu | chicken<br>鶏肉／チキン<br>toriniku/chikin |
| white meat<br>白身の肉<br>shiromi no niku | lamb<br>ラム肉<br>ramuniku | quail<br>ウズラ<br>uzura |

offal
モツ
motsu

cooked
火を通した
hi o tōshita

free-range
放し飼いの
hanashigai no

raw
生
nama

smoked
燻製の
kunsē no

organic
有機栽培の
yūkisaibai no

bacon
ベーコン
bēkon

beefburger
バーガー
bāgā

duck
鴨肉
kamoniku

ham
ハム
hamu

mince
ミンチ
minchi

ribs
スペアリブ
supearibu

sausage
ソーセージ
sōsēji

steak
ステーキ
sutēki

wagyu beef
和牛
wagyū

Fish and shellfish are a major part of the Japanese diet, whether cooked or raw as sashimi or on sushi. A huge variety of fish is eaten.

### YOU MIGHT SAY...

I'd like this filleted, please.
三枚におろしてください。
san-mai ni oroshite kudasai.

Can you cut this for sashimi, please?
刺身用に切ってください。
sashimi-yō ni kitte kudasai.

### YOU MIGHT HEAR...

Would you like this filleted?
三枚におろしましょうか。
san-mai ni oroshimashō ka?

Yes, I can do that for you.
はい、分かりました。
hai, wakarimashita.

### VOCABULARY

fishmonger
魚屋
sakana-ya

(fish)bone
骨
hone

fillet
切り身
kirimi

filleted
三枚におろした
san-mai ni oroshita

roe
卵
tamago

scales
うろこ
uroko

shellfish
貝
kai

shell
貝殻
kaigara

freshwater
淡水
tansui

saltwater
海水
kaisui

farmed
養殖の
yōshoku no

wild
養殖ではない
yōshoku dewa nai

salted
塩漬けの
shiozuke no

smoked
燻製の
kunsē no

deboned
骨を取った
hone o totta

bonito/skipjack
カツオ
katsuo

cod
タラ
tara

eel
ウナギ
unagi

flounder
ヒラメ／カレイ
hirame/karē

herring
ニシン
nishin

horse mackerel
アジ
aji

lemon sole
レモンソール
remon sōru

mackerel
サバ
saba

monkfish
アンコウ
ankō

Pacific saury
サンマ
sanma

rainbow trout
ニジマス
nijimasu

salmon
サケ
sake

sardine
イワシ
iwashi

sea bass
スズキ
suzuki

sea bream
鯛
tai

sweetfish
アユ
ayu

tuna
マグロ
maguro

yellowtail
ブリ
buri

**SEAFOOD**

abalone
アワビ
awabi

clam
アサリ
asari

crab
カニ
kani

**jellyfish**
クラゲ
kurage

**lobster**
ロブスター
robusutā

**mussel**
ムール貝
mūrugai

**octopus**
タコ
tako

**oyster**
カキ
kaki

**prawn**
海老
ebi

**scallop**
ホタテ貝
hotategai

**sea cucumber**
なまこ
namako

**sea urchin**
ウニ
uni

**shrimp**
小エビ
koebi

**spiny lobster**
伊勢海老
ise-ebi

**squid**
イカ
ika

Dairy products were only introduced in Japan in the late 19th century, and although milk is available everywhere, the range of cheeses available is limited.

## VOCABULARY

| | | |
|---|---|---|
| **cheese**<br>チーズ<br>chiizu | **semi-skimmed milk**<br>低脂肪牛乳<br>tēshibōgyūnyū | **soymilk**<br>豆乳<br>tōnyū |

**blue cheese**
ブルーチーズ
burū–chiizu

**butter**
バター
batā

**cheddar**
チェダーチーズ
chedā–chiizu

**cottage cheese**
カテージチーズ
katēji–chiizu

**cream**
クリーム
kuriimu

**egg**
卵
tamago

**milk**
牛乳／ミルク
gyūnyū/miruku

**mozzarella**
モツァレラ
motsarera

**yoghurt**
ヨーグルト
yōguruto

Gift-giving is very important in Japan. Department stores devote whole floors to gifts and wrap them beautifully to show where they were purchased.

**YOU MIGHT SAY...**

Can you gift-wrap this, please?
贈り物用に包んでください。
okurimono–yō ni tsutsunde kudasai.

**YOU MIGHT HEAR...**

Would you like this gift-wrapped?
贈り物用にお包みしましょうか。
okurimono–yō ni o–tsutsumi shimashō ka?

cotton hand towel
手ぬぐい
tenugui

Daruma doll
だるま
daruma

folding fan
扇子
sensu

lacquerware
漆塗り
urushinuri

oil-paper umbrella
和傘
wagasa

origami paper
折り紙
origami

round fan
うちわ
uchiwa

woodblock print
浮世絵
ukiyo-e

wooden doll
こけし
kokeshi

Station kiosks are handy places to buy newspapers, magazines, bento box meals, and all sorts of other useful travel essentials.

### VOCABULARY

| | | |
|---|---|---|
| tobacconist<br>タバコ屋<br>tabako-ya | tabloid<br>タブロイド紙<br>taburoidoshi | bento box<br>（お）弁当<br>(o)bentō |
| vendor<br>売り子<br>uriko | daily<br>日刊の<br>nikkan no | souvenir<br>おみやげ<br>omiyage |
| broadsheet<br>高級紙<br>kōkyūshi | weekly<br>週間の<br>shūkan no | chewing gum<br>ガム<br>gamu |

cigarette
タバコ
tabako

confectionery
菓子
kashi

energy drink
健康飲料
kenkōinryō

magazine
雑誌
zasshi

newspaper
新聞
shinbun

pen
ペン
pen

Japan is a paradise for anyone who loves stationery, from elegant traditional writing paper to cute (かわいい kawaii) designs. Handwritten letters are still valued by older generations. Instead of signatures, a seal (印鑑 inkan) with the characters for the family name is used.

envelope
封筒
fūtō

gift envelope
祝儀袋
shūgibukuro

greetings card
カード
kādo

notebook
ノート
nōto

pencil
鉛筆
enpitsu

picture postcard
絵葉書
e-hagaki

stationery
文房具
bunbōgu

sticker
シール
shiiru

writing paper
便せん
binsen

Many medicines can be bought over the counter, but others are by prescription only. Medicines in Japan are sometimes given in powder form, and it's possible to buy empty capsules and kits and fill them.

**YOU MIGHT SAY...**

I need something for...
…に効くものはありますか。
...ni kiku mono wa arimasu ka?

I'm allergic to...
…にアレルギーがあります。
...ni arerugii ga arimasu.

I'm collecting a prescription.
処方薬を取りに来ました。
shohōsen o tori ni kimashita.

What do you recommend?
何がいいですか。
nani ga ii desu ka?

Is it suitable for young children?
小さい子どもにも大丈夫ですか。
chiisai kodomo ni mo daijōbu desu ka?

**YOU MIGHT HEAR...**

Do you have a prescription?
処方箋がありますか。
shohōsen ga arimasu ka?

Do you have any allergies?
何かアレルギーがありますか。
nanika arerugii ga arimasu ka?

Take two tablets twice a day.
1日2回、2錠ずつ飲んでください。
ichi-nichi ni-jō zutsu nonde kudasai.

You should see a doctor.
お医者さんに見てもらったほうがいいですよ。
o-isha-san ni mite moratta hō ga ii desu yo.

I'd recommend...
…がいいですよ。
...ga ii desu yo.

**VOCABULARY**

| | | |
|---|---|---|
| pharmacist<br>薬剤師<br>yakuzaishi | counter<br>カウンター<br>kauntā | toiletries<br>化粧品<br>keshōhin |
| cabinet<br>陳列台<br>chinretsudai | prescription<br>処方せん<br>shohōsen | shaving foam<br>シェービングフォーム<br>shēbingu-fōmu |

| make-up remover<br>メイク落とし<br>mēku-otoshi | decongestant<br>鼻づまり薬<br>hanazumariyaku | cold<br>風邪<br>kaze |
|---|---|---|
| lip balm<br>リップクリーム<br>rippu-kuriimu | eye drops<br>目薬<br>megusuri | diarrhoea<br>下痢<br>geri |
| hairspray<br>ヘアスプレー<br>heasupurē | medicine<br>薬<br>kusuri | hayfever<br>花粉症<br>kafunshō |
| scent<br>香水<br>kōsui | painkiller<br>痛み止め<br>itamidome | headache<br>頭痛<br>zutsū |
| antihistamine<br>抗ヒスタミン<br>kō-hisutamin | tube<br>チューブ<br>chūbu | sore throat<br>のどの痛み<br>nodo no itami |

## GENERAL

antiseptic cream
殺菌クリーム
sakkin kuriimu

bandage
包帯
hōtai

capsule
カプセル
kapuseru

condom
コンドーム
kondōmu

cough mixture
咳止め
sekidome

drops
液剤
ekizai

insect repellent
虫よけ
mushi-yoke

lozenge
咳止めドロップ
sekidome doroppu

plaster
絆創膏
bansōkō

spray
スプレー
supurē

sunscreen
日焼け止め
hiyakedome

tablet/pill
錠剤
jōzai

## HYGIENE

antiperspirant
制汗剤
sēkanzai

razor
かみそり
kamisori

sanitary towel
（生理用）ナプキン
(sēri-yō) napukin

shampoo
シャンプー
shanpū

shower gel
シャワージェル
shawā jeru

soap
石鹸
sekken

tampon
タンポン

tanpon

toothbrush
歯ブラシ

haburashi

toothpaste
歯磨き粉

hamigakiko

**BEAUTY**

blusher
ほお紅

hōbeni

comb
櫛

kushi

eyeliner
アイライナー

airainā

eyeshadow
アイシャドー

aishadō

foundation
ファンデーション

fandēshon

hairbrush
ヘアブラシ

heaburashi

lipstick
口紅

kuchibeni

mascara
マスカラ

masukara

nail varnish
マニキュア

manikyua

107

## VOCABULARY

| | | |
|---|---|---|
| dummy<br>おしゃぶり<br>oshaburi | to be teething<br>歯が生える<br>ha ga haeru | to breast-feed<br>授乳する<br>junyū suru |

## CLOTHING

baby shoes
ベビーシューズ
bebii–shūzu

bib
よだれ掛け
yodare kake

bodysuit
ロンパース
ronpāsu

hat
帽子
bōshi

mittens
ミトン
miton

vest
シャツ
shatsu

## HEALTH AND HYGIENE

baby food
ベビーフード
bebii fūdo

baby's bottle
哺乳瓶
honyūbin

changing bag
ベビーバッグ
bebii baggu

cotton bud
綿棒
menbō

formula milk
粉ミルク
kona miruku

nappy
おむつ
omutsu

nappy cream
おむつ用クリーム
omutsu-yō kuriimu

potty
幼児用おまる
yōji-yō omaru

wet wipes
ウエットティッシュ
uetto-tisshu

## ACCESSORIES

baby seat
チャイルドシート
chairudo shiito

baby sling
抱っこひも
dakkohimo

cot
ベビーベッド
bebii beddo

highchair
ハイチェア
haichea

pram
乳母車
ubaguruma

pushchair
ベビーカー
bebiikā

Department stores usually open from 10 a.m. to 8 p.m., including Sundays, but close on one day during the week.

### YOU MIGHT SAY...

Where is...?
…はどこですか。
...wa doko desu ka?

Which floor is this?
ここは何階ですか。
koko wa nan-gai desu ka?

### YOU MIGHT HEAR...

Menswear is on the second floor.
紳士服売り場は3階です。
shinshi-fuku uriba wa san-gai desu.

This is the first floor.
ここは2階です。
koko wa ni-kai desu.

### VOCABULARY

brand
ブランド
burando

counter
カウンター
kauntā

department
売り場
uriba

... floor
…かい／がい
... kai/gai

escalator
エスカレーター
esukarētā

lift
エレベーター
erebētā

toilets
トイレ／お手洗い
toire/otearai

sale
売出し
uridashi

sales tax refund
counter
免税カウンター
menzē kauntā

women's/men's/
children's clothing
婦人／紳士／子供
服
fujin-/shinshi-/kodomo-
fuku

sportswear
スポーツウェア
supōtsu-wea

swimwear
水着
mizugi

coffee shop
喫茶店
kissaten

### YOU SHOULD KNOW...

Overseas visitors can get sales tax refunded by showing their passports at a dedicated counter. Some other tourist-oriented shops offer this too.

accessories
装飾品
sōshokuhin

bags
かばん
kaban

cosmetics
化粧品
keshōhin

electronics
家電
kaden

fashion
ファッション
fasshon

food and drink
食品
shokuhin

footwear
靴
kutsu

furniture
家具
kagu

gifts
ギフト
gifuto

homeware
インテリア
interia

lingerie
下着／肌着
shitagi/hadagi

toys
おもちゃ
omocha

Larger sizes of clothing and shoes are not available everywhere, and the Japanese fit may not suit Western figures or feet.

**YOU MIGHT SAY...**

I'd like to try this on, please.
これを試着してみたいんですが。
kore o shichaku shite mitai n desu ga.

Where are the fitting rooms?
試着室はどこですか。
shichakushitsu wa doko desu ka?

I'm a size...
私のサイズは…です。
watashi no saizu wa ...desu.

Have you got a bigger/smaller size?
もっと大きい／小さいのはありますか。
motto ōkii/chiisai no wa arimasu ka?

This is too small/big.
これは小さすぎます／大きすぎます。
kore wa chiisasugimasu/ōkisugimasu.

This is torn.
破れています。
yaburete imasu.

It's not my style.
私のスタイルじゃありません。
watashi no sutairu ja arimasen.

**YOU MIGHT HEAR...**

Let me know if I can help.
御用があれば、声をおかけください。
go-yō ga areba, koe o o-kake kudasai.

The fitting rooms are over there.
試着室はあちらです。
shichakushitsu wa achira desu.

What size are you?
サイズはいくつですか。
saizu wa ikutsu desu ka.

I'm sorry, it's out of stock.
すみません、売り切れました。
sumimasen, urikiremashita.

I'm sorry, we don't have that size/colour.
申し訳ありません。そのサイズ／色はございません。
mōshiwake arimasen. sono saizu/iro wa gozaimasen.

That suits you.
お似合いですよ。
o-niai desu yo.

## VOCABULARY

| | | |
|---|---|---|
| fitting room<br>試着室<br>shichakushitsu | jewellery<br>アクセサリー<br>akusesarii | denim<br>デニム<br>denimu |
| size<br>サイズ<br>saizu | umbrella<br>傘<br>kasa | cotton<br>綿<br>men |
| clothes/clothing<br>服<br>fuku | casual<br>カジュアルな<br>kajuaruna | leather<br>皮革<br>hikaku |
| shoes<br>靴<br>kutsu | smart<br>きちんとした<br>kichinto shita | silk<br>絹<br>kinu |
| underwear<br>下着<br>shitagi | wool<br>ウール<br>ūru | to try on<br>試着する<br>shichaku suru |

## YOU SHOULD KNOW...

Traditional Japanese formal clothing includes the kimono, sash, kimono jacket, thonged sandals, and split-toe socks. In winter, padded indoor jackets (はんてん hanten) are great in older houses without central heating.

## JAPANESE CLOTHING

cotton summer kimono
浴衣
yukata

happi festival coat
はっぴ
happi

kimono
着物
kimono

sash
帯
obi

split-toe socks
足袋
tabi

wooden clogs
下駄
geta

blouse
ブラウス
burausu

boxer shorts
パンツ
pantsu

bra
ブラ
bura

cardigan
カーディガン
kādigan

coat
コート
kōto

dress (casual)
ワンピース
wanpiisu

dress (formal)
ドレス
doresu

jacket
上着
uwagi

jeans
ジーンズ
jiinzu

jogging bottoms
ジョギングパンツ
jogingu-pantsu

jumper
セーター
sētā

leggings
スパッツ
supattsu

pants
パンティー
pantii

pyjamas
パジャマ
pajama

shirt
シャツ
shatsu

shorts
ショーツ
shōtsu

skirt
スカート
sukāto

socks
靴下
kutsushita

sweatshirt
トレーナー
torēnā

suit
スーツ
sūtsu

tights
タイツ
taitsu

trousers
ズボン／パンツ
zubon/pantsu

T-shirt
Tシャツ
tii-shatsu

waterproof jacket
防水ジャケット
bōsui-jaketto

## ACCESSORIES

belt
ベルト
beruto

bracelet
ブレスレット
buresuretto

earrings
イヤリング
iyaringu

gloves
手袋
tebukuro

handbag
ハンドバッグ
handobaggu

necklace
ネックレス
nekkuresu

purse
財布
saifu

scarf
マフラー
mafurā

tie
ネクタイ
nekutai

boots
ブーツ
būtsu

court shoes
パンプス
panpusu

high heels
ハイヒール
hai-hēru

lace-up shoes
靴ひも付きの靴
kutsuhimo tsuki no kutsu

sandals
サンダル
sandaru

slippers
スリッパ
surippa

walking boots
トレッキングシューズ
torekkingu shūzu

trainers
スニーカー
suniikā

Wellington boots
長靴
nagagutsu

## VOCABULARY

tool
道具
dōgu

stepladder
踏み台
fumidai

to renovate
改装／リフォームする
kaisō/rifōmu suru

toolbox
道具箱
dōgubako

to do DIY
日曜大工をする
nichiyōdaiku o suru

hammer
かなづち
kanazuchi

nails
くぎ
kugi

paint
ペンキ
penki

paintbrush
ペンキブラシ
penki burashi

saw
のこぎり
nokogiri

screwdriver
ドライバー
doraibā

screws
スクリュー
sukuryū

spanner
スパナ
supana

wallpaper
壁紙
kabegami

Japan's discount shops, called "100-yen shops" (百円ショップ hyaku-en shoppu), are treasure troves of bargain goods of all kinds for the home, as well as stationery, sports items, and so on.

**antiques shop**
骨とう品屋
kottōhin-ya

**barber's**
床屋
tokoya

**bookshop**
本屋
hon-ya

**discount shop**
100円ショップ
hyaku-en shoppu

**electrical store**
電気屋
denki-ya

**electronics store**
家電販売店
kaden hanbaiten

florist's
花屋
hana-ya

furniture store
家具屋
kagu-ya

hairdresser's/beauty salon
美容院
biyōin

health food shop
健康食品店
kenkō shokuhinten

jeweller's
貴金属店
kikinzokuten

music shop
ミュージックショップ
myūjikku-shoppu

off-licence
酒屋
saka-ya

optician's
眼鏡屋
megane-ya

pet shop
ペットショップ
pettoshoppu

shoe shop
靴屋
kutsu-ya

toyshop
おもちゃ屋
omocha-ya

travel agency
旅行代理店
ryokō dairiten

# DAY-TO-DAY | 日常生活

Studying, business meetings, or meals with friends... whatever your day-to-day schedule looks like during your time in Japan, you will require some basic vocabulary when going on errands, planning outings, and going about your everyday business.

**white coffee**
カフェオーレ
kafeōre

**handle**
取手
totte

**cup**
カップ
kappu

**saucer**
受け皿
ukezara

## YOU MIGHT SAY...

Where are you going?
どこにお出かけですか。
doko ni o-dekake desu ka?

What time do you finish?
何時に終わりますか。
nan-ji ni owarimasu ka?

What are you doing today/tonight?
今日／今晩、何をしますか。
kyō/konban nani o shimasu ka?

Are you free on Friday?
金曜日は暇ですか。
kin'yōbi wa hima desu ka?

Where/When would you like to meet?
どこで／いつ、会いましょうか。
doko de/itsu aimashō ka?

## YOU MIGHT HEAR...

I'm at work/university.
働いています／大学で勉強しています。
hataraite imasu/daigaku de benkyō shite imasu.

I have a day off.
休みです。
yasumi desu.

I'm going to...
…に行きます。
...ni ikimasu.

I'll be back by...
…までに戻ります。
...made ni modorimasu.

I'll meet you at the restaurant.
レストランで会いましょう。
resutoran de aimashō.

## VOCABULARY

to wake up
目が覚める
me ga sameru

to get dressed
服を着る
fuku o kiru

to eat
食べる
taberu

to drink
飲む
nomu

to study
勉強する
benkyō suru

to work
働く
hataraku

to meet friends
友達に会う
tomodachi ni au

to go home
家に帰る
ie ni kaeru

to go to bed
寝る
neru

A traditional Japanese breakfast is a smaller, simpler version of a main meal, with rice, miso soup, grilled fish or egg, vegetables or pickles, accompanied by green tea. Western-style breakfasts are becoming increasingly popular, and coffee shops often offer a set breakfast deal called モーニング・サービス (mōningu sābisu – literally "morning service") or モーニング・セット (mōningu setto). This comprises thickly sliced buttered white toast, hard-boiled egg, mini-salad, and tea or coffee.

## VOCABULARY

| to have breakfast | to skip breakfast |
|---|---|
| 朝ごはんを食べる | 朝ごはんを抜く |
| asagohan o taberu | asagohan o nuku |

## YOU SHOULD KNOW...

There are set phrases to say before and after eating: いただきます (itadakimasu) and ごちそうさま (gochisōsama), which mean roughly: "I humbly eat" and "It was a lovely meal".

bread
パン
pan

black tea
紅茶
kōcha

cereal
シリアル
shiriaru

coffee
コーヒー
kōhii

croissant
クロワッサン
kurowassan

fermented soy beans
納豆
nattō

green tea
お茶／煎茶
o-cha/sencha

grilled fish
焼き魚
yakizakana

hard-boiled egg
ゆで卵
yude–tamago

jam
ジャム
jamu

miso soup
みそ汁
misoshiru

orange juice
オレンジジュース
orenji jūsu

pickled plums
梅干し
umeboshi

rice porridge
お粥
o-kayu

rolled omelette
卵焼き
tamagoyaki

toast
トースト
tōsuto

white coffee
カフェオーレ
kafeōre

yoghurt
ヨーグルト
yōguruto

Japanese meals often consist of several dishes served at the same time, rather than a sequence of courses. Desserts are not a traditional part of Japanese meals, but a piece of fruit might be prepared and served.

**YOU MIGHT SAY...**

What's for dinner?
晩ご飯は何ですか。
bangohan wa nan desu ka?

What time is lunch?
昼ご飯は何時ですか。
hirugohan wa nan-ji desu ka?

May I have ..., please?
…をお願いします。
...o onegai shimasu.

Can I try it?
味見してもいいですか。
ajimi shite mo ii desu ka?

**YOU MIGHT HEAR...**

We're having ... for dinner.
晩ご飯は…です。
bangohan wa ...desu.

Lunch is at midday.
昼ご飯は正午です。
hirugohan wa shōgo desu.

Dinner's ready!
晩ご飯ができましたよ!
bangohan ga dekimashita yo.

Would you like...?
…はいかがですか。
...wa ikaga desu ka?

**VOCABULARY**

| | | |
|---|---|---|
| food | lunch | to have lunch |
| 食べ物 | 昼ご飯 | 昼ご飯を食べる |
| tabemono | hirugohan | hiru-gohan o taberu |
| drink | dinner | to have dinner |
| 飲み物 | 晩ご飯 | 晩ご飯を食べる |
| nomimono | bangohan | ban-gohan o taberu |

**YOU SHOULD KNOW...**

Rice is at the heart of the Japanese diet and culture, and is strongly associated with Shinto and symbolic of prosperity. While the plant and uncooked rice are called 米 (kome), cooked rice served in Japanese or Chinese style is called ご飯 (gohan). Gohan means "meal" or "food", for example, breakfast (朝ご飯 asagohan), and evening meal (晩ご飯 bangohan). Rice cooked in other styles, for example with curry, is called ライス (raisu).

beef cooked in stock
with dipping sauce
しゃぶしゃぶ
shabu–shabu

beef hotpot cooked in
sweetened stock
すき焼き
sukiyaki

breaded pork cutlet
トンカツ
tonkatsu

buckwheat noodles
そば
soba

chicken and egg on rice
親子丼
oyako–don

Chinese noodles
ラーメン
rāmen

Chinese-style
dumplings
餃子
gyōza

curry with rice
カレーライス
karēraisu

grilled eel on rice
うな重
una–jū

Japanese hotpot
ちゃんこ鍋
chanko nabe

Japanese-style rice
ご飯
gohan

miso soup
みそ汁
misoshiru

sashimi
刺身
sashimi

savoury egg custard
茶碗蒸し
chawan mushi

stir-fried Chinese noodles
with meat and vegetables
焼きそば
yakisoba

sushi
すし
sushi

tempura
てんぷら
tenpura

wheat noodles
うどん
udon

**WESTERN DISHES**

chips
フライドポテト
furaido poteto

cooked vegetables
温野菜
on-yasai

gratin
グラタン
guratan

omelette
オムレツ
omuretsu

pasta
パスタ
pasuta

pizza
ピザ
piza

potatoes
ジャガイモ
jagaimo

raw vegetables
生野菜
nama-yasai

salad
サラダ
sarada

## SNACKS AND SWEET THINGS

azuki bean jelly
ようかん
yōkan

coffee jelly
コーヒーゼリー
kōhii zerii

crème caramel
プリン
purin

flavoured shaved ice
かき氷
kakigōri

fruit parfait
フルーツパフェ
furūtsu pafe

ice cream
アイスクリーム
aisukuriimu

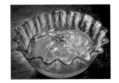

seaweed jelly
ところてん
tokoroten

sponge cake
カステラ
kasutera

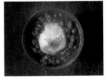

sweet azuki bean soup
お汁粉
oshiruko

Japanese restaurants often specialize in one type of food, for example, tempura, sushi, and are described accordingly as "... shop": 天ぷらや (tenpura-ya), 寿司屋 (sushi-ya). Many restaurants and cafés have window displays of plastic food, useful if you can't read the menu. In some traditional restaurants, you leave your shoes outside the dining room and sit on cushions on the tatami-mat floor at a low table. Most coffee shops and restaurants will bring you a glass of water or a cup of green tea, and an おしぼり (o-shibori) – a small, moist towel – to wipe your hands.

## YOU MIGHT SAY...

I'd like to make a reservation.
予約をしたいんですが。
yoyaku shitai n desu ga.

A table for four, please.
4人、お願いします。
yo-nin onegai shimasu.

A non-smoking table, please.
禁煙席、お願いします。
kin'en-seki onegai shimasu.

We're ready to order.
注文が決まりました。
chūmon ga kimarimashite.

What would you recommend?
お薦めは何ですか。
o-susume wa nan desu ka?

What are the specials today?
今日のお薦めは何ですか。
kyō no o-susume wa nan desu ka?

May I have ..., please?
…をお願いします。
...o onegai shimasu.

Are there vegetarian/vegan options?
ベジタリアン用／ビーガン用
にできますか。
bejitarian-/biigan-yō ni dekimasu ka?

I'm allergic to...
…にアレルギーがあります。
...ni arerugii ga arimasu.

Cheers!
乾杯!
kanpai!

Excuse me, this is cold/too salty.
すみませんが、これは冷たい
です／しょっぱすぎます。
sumimasen ga, kore wa tsumetai desu/shoppasugimasu.

This is not what I ordered.
注文したものと違います。
chūmon shita mono to chigaimasu.

May we have the bill, please?
お勘定、お願いします。
o-kanjō, onegai shimasu.

| | |
|---|---|
| At what time?<br>何時ですか。<br>nan-ji desu ka? | Are you ready to order?<br>ご注文はお決まりですか。<br>go-chūmon wa o-kimari desu ka? |
| For how many people?<br>何名様ですか。<br>nan-mē-sama desu ka? | I would recommend...<br>…がお薦めです。<br>...ga o-susume desu. |
| Would you like anything to drink?<br>お飲み物はいかがですか。<br>o-nomimono wa ikaga desu ka? | The specials today are...<br>本日のお薦めは…です。<br>honjitsu no o-susume wa ...desu. |

**VOCABULARY**

| | | |
|---|---|---|
| bar<br>バー<br>bā | daily specials<br>今日のお薦め<br>kyō no o-susume | vegetarian<br>ベジタリアン用<br>bejitarian-yō |
| café/coffee shop<br>喫茶店<br>kissaten | set menu<br>セット<br>setto | vegan<br>ビーガン用<br>biigan-yō |
| pub<br>居酒屋<br>izakaya | service charge<br>サービス料<br>sābisu-ryō | to reserve a table<br>席を予約する<br>seki o yoyaku suru |
| restaurant<br>レストラン<br>resutoran | tip<br>チップ<br>chippu | to order<br>注文する<br>chūmon suru |

**YOU SHOULD KNOW...**

An 居酒屋 (izakaya) serves sake 酒, Japanese lager-style beer, Japanese spirits (焼酎 shochū), soft drinks, and small reasonably-priced dishes. Bars focus more on the alcohol, from beer to cocktails and spirits.

ashtray
灰皿
haizara

beer mug
ジョッキ
jokki

bill
お勘定
o-kanjō

chair
椅子
isu

chopsticks
箸
hashi

chopstick rest
箸置き
hashi-oki

floor cushion
座布団
zabuton

glass
コップ
koppu

Japanese teacup
湯呑茶碗
yunomijawan

knife and fork
ナイフとフォーク
naifu to fōku

low table
座卓
zataku

menu
メニュー
menyū

miso soup bowl
おわん
o-wan

moist towel
おしぼり
o-shibori

plate
皿
sara

rice bowl
茶碗
chawan

sake cup and flask
おちょことっくり
o-choko to tokkuri

salt and pepper
塩とこしょう
shio to koshō

soy sauce
醤油
shōyu

spoon
スプーン
supūn

table
テーブル
tēburu

toothpicks
つまようじ
tsumayōji

waiter/waitress
ウェイター/
ウェイトレス
weitā/weitoresu

wine glass
ワイングラス
wain-gurasu

Burgers and other American-style food can be found across Japan, and are popular in various fast-food chains.

### YOU MIGHT SAY...

I'd like to order, please.
注文おねがいします。
chūmon onegai shimasu.

Do you deliver?
配達してもらえますか。
haitatsu shite moraemasu ka?

### YOU MIGHT HEAR...

Sit-in or takeaway?
お召し上がりですか。お持ち帰りですか。
o-meshiagari desu ka? o-mochikaeri desu ka?

Would you like anything else?
他にご注文は？
hoka ni go-chūmon wa?

### VOCABULARY

food stall
屋台
yatai

vendor
売り子
uriko

drive-thru
ドライブスルー
doraibusurū

takeaway food
持ち帰り
mochikaeri

to order
注文する
chūmon suru

to deliver
配達する
haitatsu suru

### YOU SHOULD KNOW...

More traditional Japanese fast food ranges from a quick bowl of noodles to sushi and pot noodles from convenience stores.

bento box
（お）弁当
(o)bentō

burger
バーガー
bāgā

chicken yakitori
焼き鳥
yakitori

fried tofu and rice balls
いなりずし
inari-zushi

fries
フレンチフライ
furenchi-furai

hot dog
ホットドッグ
hottodoggu

Japanese stew
おでん
oden

maki rolls
巻きずし
maki-zushi

octopus dumplings
たこやき
takoyaki

onigiri
おにぎり
onigiri

sandwich
サンドイッチ
sandoitchi

steamed stuffed bun
肉まん
nikuman

sushi
すし
sushi

toasted sandwich
ホットサンド
hotto sando

vending machine
自動販売機
jidōhanbaiki

Technology plays a huge role in people's everyday lives. A mere click, tap, or swipe helps us to stay in touch with friends and family, keep up to date with what's going on, and find the information we need.

## YOU MIGHT SAY/HEAR...

I'll phone you later.
後で電話します。
ato de denwa shimasu.

What's your number?
電話番号は何ですか。
denwa bangō wa nan desu ka?

I'll email you.
メールを送りますね。
mēru o okurimasu ne.

The website address is...
ホームページアドレスは…です。
hōmupēji adoresu wa ...desu.

Can I call you back?
後で、かけ直してもいいですか。
ato de kakenaoshite mo ii desu ka?

What's the WiFi password?
Wifi のパスワードは何ですか。
waifai no pasuwādo wa nan desu ka?

I don't have any signal.
圏外です。
kengai desu.

It's all one word.
ひと続きです
hitotsuzuki desu

## VOCABULARY

social media
ソーシャルメディア
sōsharu media

email
メール
mēru

website
(ウェブ)サイト
(webu)saito

app
アプリ
apuri

email address
メールアドレス
mēru adoresu

link
リンク
rinku

internet
インターネット
intānetto

WiFi
Wifi
waifai

icon
アイコン
aikon

| | | |
|---|---|---|
| touchscreen<br>タッチスクリーン<br>tatchisukuriin | mobile phone<br>携帯（電話）<br>kētai (denwa) | to make a phone call<br>電話をかける<br>denwa o kakeru |
| mouse<br>マウス<br>mausu | landline<br>固定電話<br>kotē denwa | to charge a mobile<br>携帯を充電する<br>kētai o jūden suru |
| keyboard<br>キーボード<br>kiibōdo | battery<br>乾電池<br>kandenchi | to send an email<br>メールを送る<br>mēru o okuru |
| screen<br>モニター<br>monitā | phone signal<br>電話信号<br>denwa shingō | to download/upload<br>ダウンロードする/<br>アップロードする<br>daunrōdo suru/<br>appurōdo suru |
| data<br>データ<br>dēta | voice mail<br>音声メール<br>onsē-mēru | to log on/off<br>ログイン／オフする<br>rogu in/ofu suru |

---

**YOU SHOULD KNOW...**

---

There are no pay-as-you-go mobiles, and contracts are only available for residents. SMS texts aren't used; instead, mobiles have dedicated email addresses.

Bluetooth® headset
ブルートゥース™ヘ
ッドセット
burūtūsu heddosetto

charger
チャージャー
chājā

computer
コンピュータ
konpyūta

mouse mat
マウスパッド
mausu paddo

phone case
携帯カバー
kētai kabā

power pack
モバイルパワーパック
mobairu pawāpakku

SIM card
SIM カード
shimu kādo

smartphone
スマートフォン
sumātofon

tablet
タブレット
taburetto

wireless router
無線ルーター
musen rūtā

The Japanese school system is based on the American one: elementary school from age 6 to 12, junior high from 12 to 15, senior high from 15 to 18, followed by four-year university degrees or two years at junior college or vocational college. Daycare centres and nurseries cater for younger children.

## YOU MIGHT SAY...

What are you studying?
何を勉強していますか。
nani o benkyō shite imasu ka?

What year are you in?
何年生ですか。
nan-nensē desu ka?

What's your favourite subject?
好きな科目は何ですか。
suki-na kamoku wa nan desu ka?

## YOU MIGHT HEAR...

I'm studying...
…を勉強しています。
...o benkyō shite imasu.

I'm in second year at university.
大学2年生です。
daigaku ni-nensē desu.

I enjoy...
…が大好きです。
...ga dai-suki desu.

## VOCABULARY

nursery
保育園
hoikuen

elementary school
小学校
shōgakkō

junior high school
中学校
chūgakkō

senior high school
高校
kōkō

college
短大
tandai

university
大学
daigaku

headteacher
校長
kōchō

teacher
教師／先生
kyōshi/sensē

caretaker
用務員
yōmuin

pupil
生徒
sēto

timetable
時間割
jikanwari

lesson
授業
jugyō

| lecture<br>講義<br>kōgi | postgraduate<br>大学院生<br>daigakuinsē | overseas student<br>留学生<br>ryūgakusē |
|---|---|---|
| tutorial<br>個別指導<br>kobetsu shidō | classroom<br>教室<br>kyōshitsu | to learn<br>学ぶ<br>manabu |
| assignment<br>研究課題<br>kenkyū-kadai | assembly hall<br>講堂<br>kōdō | to teach<br>教える<br>oshieru |
| homework<br>宿題<br>shukudai | playing field<br>校庭<br>kōtē | to revise<br>復習する<br>fukushū suru |
| exam<br>試験<br>shiken | halls of residence<br>大学寮<br>daigakuryō | to sit an exam<br>試験を受ける<br>shiken o ukeru |
| degree<br>学位<br>gakui | student union<br>学生自治会<br>gakusē-jichikai | to graduate<br>卒業する<br>sotsugyō suru |
| undergraduate<br>学部学生<br>gakubu-gakusē | student card<br>学生証<br>gakusēshō | to study<br>勉強する<br>benkyō suru |

**SCHOOL**

---

blackboard
黒板
kokuban

calculator
計算機
keisan ki

colouring pencils
色鉛筆
iro-enpitsu

eraser
消しゴム
keshigomu

exercise book
練習帳
renshū-chō

highlighter
蛍光ペン
kēkō-pen

hole punch
穴あけパンチ
ana-ake-panchi

Japanese abacus
そろばん
soroban

mechanical pencil
シャープペン
shāpupen

paper
紙
kami

pen
ペン
pen

pencil
鉛筆
enpitsu

pencil case
ペンケース
pen-kēsu

ring binder
バインダー
baindā

ruler
物差し
monosashi

satchel
ランドセル
randoseru

schoolbag
学生かばん
gakusē-kaban

scissors
はさみ
hasami

sharpener
鉛筆削り
enpitsu kezuri

textbook
教科書
kyōkasho

whiteboard
ホワイトボード
howaitobōdo

## HIGHER EDUCATION

cafeteria
学食
gakushoku

campus
キャンパス
kyanpasu

lecture hall
階段教室
kaidan-kyōshitsu

lecturer
講師
kōshi

library
図書館
toshokan

student
学生
gakusē

Office hours are usually 9 a.m. to 5.30 p.m., Monday to Friday, but working long hours of overtime is expected in many workplaces. Paid holiday days are fewer than in the UK and many workers don't take their full quota. However, taking an hour's lunch break between 12 noon and 1 p.m. is the norm.

## YOU MIGHT SAY/HEAR...

Can we arrange a meeting?
打ち合わせをしましょうか。
uchiawase o shimashō ka?

I have a meeting with...
…さんと打ち合わせがあります。
...san to uchiawase ga arimasu.

Are you free this afternoon?
午後、時間がありますか。
gogo, jikan ga arimasu ka?

I'll email the files to you.
ファイルをメールで送ります。
fairu o mēru de okurimasu.

May I speak to...?
…とお話ができますか。
...to o-hanashi ga dekimasu ka?

Here's my business card.
私の名刺です。
watashi no mēshi desu.

Can you send me...?
…を送ってください。
...o okutte kudasai.

Who's calling?
どちら様でしょうか。
dochira-sama deshō ka?

## VOCABULARY

| | | |
|---|---|---|
| manager<br>主任<br>shunin | client<br>顧客<br>kokyaku | accounts<br>会計<br>kaikē |
| staff<br>スタッフ<br>sutaffu | supplier<br>納入業者<br>nōnyūgyōsha | figures<br>数字<br>sūji |
| colleague<br>同僚<br>dōryō | human resources<br>人事部<br>jinji-bu | spreadsheet<br>スプレッドシート<br>supureddoshiito |

| | | |
|---|---|---|
| presentation<br>プレゼン<br>purezen | file<br>ファイル<br>fairu | wireless<br>ワイヤレス<br>waiyaresu |
| report<br>報告<br>hōkoku | attachment<br>添付ファイル<br>tenpu-fairu | to type<br>タイプする<br>taipu suru |
| meeting<br>会議<br>kaigi | inbox<br>受信トレイ<br>jushin-torei | to give a presentation<br>プレゼンをする<br>purezen o suru |
| conference call<br>電話会議<br>denwa-kaigi | username<br>ユーザー名<br>yūzāmē | to hold a meeting<br>会議を持つ<br>kaigi o motsu |
| video conference<br>テレビ会議<br>terebi-kaigi | password<br>パスワード<br>pasuwādo | to Skype®<br>スカイプ®をする<br>sukaipu o suru |

desk
机
tsukue

desk lamp
電気スタンド
denki-sutando

filing cabinet
ファイリングキャビ
ネット
fairingu kyabinetto

folder
フォルダー
forudā

ink cartridge
インクカートリッジ
inku kātoridji

in/out tray
決裁箱
kessaibako

**laptop**
ノートパソコン／ラップトップ
nōto pasokon/rapputoppu

**notepad**
メモ帳
memochō

**paper clip**
ゼムクリップ
zemukurippu

**photocopier**
コピー機
kopiiki

**printer**
プリンター
purintā

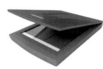
**scanner**
スキャナ
sukyana

**stapler**
ホチキス™
hochikisu

**sticky notes**
付箋
fusen

**sticky tape**
セロテープ™
serotēpu

**swivel chair**
回転いす
kaiten-isu

**telephone**
電話
denwa

**USB stick**
USB メモリ
yū-esu-bii memori

Japan is still mainly a cash economy, but many large shops, hotels, and restaurants will accept cards. Some ATMs allow cash withdrawals for most non-Japanese debit/credit cards – check if the machine has an "International ATM Service".

## YOU MIGHT SAY...

I'd like to...
…たいんですが。
...tai n desu ga.

... open an account.
銀行口座を開き…
ginkō-kōza o hiraki...

... register for online banking.
インターネットバンキングの登録がし…
intānetto-bankingu no tōroku ga shi...

Is there a fee for this service?
手数料がかかりますか。
tesūryō ga kakarimasu ka?

I need to cancel my debit/credit card.
デビット/クレジットカードをキャンセルしなければなりません。
debitto/kurejitto kādo o kyanseru shinakereba narimasen.

I'd like to change £100.
100ポンド、両替したいんですが。
hyaku-pondo, ryōgae shitai n desu ga.

## YOU MIGHT HEAR...

May I see your ID, please?
身分証明書を見せていただけますか。
mibun-shōmēsho o misete itadakemasu ka?

How much would you like to withdraw/deposit?
いくらお引出し／お預けになりますか。
ikura o-hikidashi/o-azuke ni narimasu ka?

Could you enter your PIN, please?
暗証番号をご入力ください。
anshō-bangō o go-nyūryoku kudasai.

You must fill out an application form.
申し込み用紙にご記入ください。
mōshikomi-yōshi ni go-kinyū kudasai.

branch
支店
shiten

account number
口座番号
kōzabangō

currency
通貨
tsūka

cashier
出納係
suitōgakari

bank balance
銀行預金残高
ginkō-yokin zandaka

to borrow
借りる
kariru

online banking
インターネットバン
キング
intānetto-bankingu

overdraft
当座貸越
tōza kashikoshi

to withdraw
お金をおろす
okane o orosu

bank account
銀行口座
ginkō kōza

interest
利子
rishi

to make a deposit
預金する
yokin suru

current/savings account
当座預金/普通預金
tōzayokin/futsūyokin

bank transfer
銀行振込
ginkō furikomi

to change money
両替する
ryōgae suru

account passbook
貯金通帳
chokin tsūchō

ATM
ATM
ē-tii-emu

banknotes
紙幣
shihē

bureau de change
両替所
ryōgaejo

debit/credit card
デビット/クレジッ
トカード
debitto/kurejitto kādo

exchange rate
両替率
ryōgaeritsu

Post offices are usually open 9 a.m. to 5 p.m., Monday to Friday. Some post offices in the main cities stay open until around 7 p.m. and at weekends.

## YOU MIGHT SAY...

I'd like to send this by airmail/surface mail.
これを航空便／船便で送りたいんですが。
kore o kōkūbin/funabin de okuritai n desu ga.

Can I get a certificate of postage, please?
書留にしてください。
kakitome ni shite kudasai.

How long will delivery take?
届くのにどのぐらいかかりますか。
todoku no ni dono gurai kakarimasu ka?

I'd like to buy ... stamps, please.
切手を…枚ください。
kitte o ...mai kudasai.

## YOU MIGHT HEAR...

Place it on the scales, please.
はかりに載せてください。
hakari ni nosete kudasai.

What are the contents?
中身は何ですか。
nakami wa nan desu ka?

Would you like a certificate of postage?
配達証明は要りますか。
haitatsu-shōmē wa irimasu ka?

How many stamps do you require?
切手は何枚でしょうか。
kitte wa nan-mai deshō ka?

Please fill in this form.
この用紙に記入してください。
kono yōshi ni kinyū shite kudasai.

## YOU SHOULD KNOW...

You can withdraw money with your non-Japanese credit or debit card at post office ATMs. A single transaction withdrawal is limited to 50,000 yen.

## VOCABULARY

| | | |
|---|---|---|
| address | postcode | courier |
| 住所 | 郵便番号 | 宅配業者 |
| jūsho | yūbin-bangō | takuhai gyōsha |

| mail | express delivery | to receive mail |
|---|---|---|
| 郵便<br>yūbin | 速達<br>sokutatsu | 郵便を受け取る<br>yūbin o uketoru |

| surface mail | to post | to return a package |
|---|---|---|
| 船便<br>funabin | 投函する<br>tōkan suru | 小包を送り返す<br>kozutsumi o okurikaesu |

| airmail | to send | to deliver |
|---|---|---|
| 航空便<br>kōkūbin | 送る<br>okuru | 配達する<br>haitatsu suru |

box
箱
hako

envelope
封筒
fūtō

letter
手紙
tegami

package
小包
kozutsumi

padded envelope
クッション封筒
kusshon-fūtō

picture postcard
絵葉書
e-hagaki

postal worker
郵便局員
yūbinkyokuin

postbox
郵便ポスト
yūbin posto

stamp
切手
kitte

## YOU MIGHT SAY...

How do I get to the city centre?
どうやって町の中心に行けますか。
dō yatte machi no chūshin ni ikemasu ka?

I'd like to visit...
…に行きたいです。
...ni ikitai desu.

I need to go to...
…に行かなければいけません。
...ni ikanakereba ikemasen.

What are the opening hours?
営業時間は何時から何時までですか。
ēgyō jikan wa nan-ji kara nan-ji made desu ka?

## YOU MIGHT HEAR...

It's open between ... and...
…時から…時まで開いています。
... ji kara ... ji made aite imasu.

It's closed on Mondays.
月曜日は休みです。
getsuyōbi wa yasumi desu.

Buddhist temple
お寺
o-tera

café/coffee shop
喫茶店
kissaten

church
教会
kyōkai

city hall
市役所
shiyakusho

community police post
交番
kōban

conference centre
会議場
kaigijō

courthouse
裁判所
saibansho

fire station
消防署
shōbōsho

hospital
病院
byōin

hotel
ホテル
hoteru

laundrette
コインランドリー
koin-randorii

library
図書館
toshokan

mosque
モスク
mosuku

office block
オフィスビル
ofisu-biru

park
公園
kōen

playground
遊び場
asobiba

police station
警察署
kēsatsusho

Shinto shrine
神社
jinja

# LEISURE | 余暇

A day trip, a break away, a night out, maybe even a night in – we all like to spend our free time differently. It's also a common topic of conversation with friends and colleagues; who doesn't like talking about holidays, hobbies, and how they like to hang out?

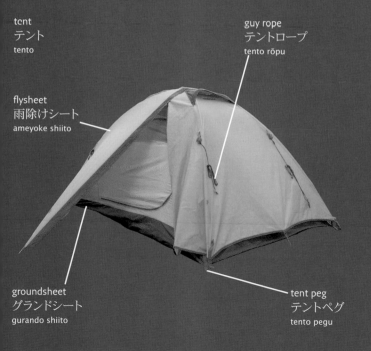

tent
テント
tento

guy rope
テントロープ
tento rōpu

flysheet
雨除けシート
ameyoke shiito

groundsheet
グランドシート
gurando shiito

tent peg
テントペグ
tento pegu

## YOU MIGHT SAY...

What would you like to do?
何がしたいですか。
nani ga shitai desu ka?

What do you do in your spare time?
暇な時、何をしますか。
hima-na toki nani o shimasu ka?

Have you got any hobbies?
趣味はありますか。
shumi wa arimasu ka?

Do you enjoy...?
…が好きですか。
...ga suki desu ka?

Are you sporty/musical?
スポーツ／音楽が得意ですか。
supōtsu/ongaku ga tokui desu ka?

Are you going on holiday this year?
今年、どこかに休暇で行きますか。
kotoshi, dokoka ni kyūka de ikimasu ka?

## YOU MIGHT HEAR...

My hobbies are...
趣味は ... です。
shumi wa... desu.

I like...
…が好きです。
...ga suki desu.

I really enjoy it.
とても楽しいです。
totemo tanoshii desu.

It's not for me.
私の趣味じゃありません。
watashi no shumi ja arimasen.

I am/I am not sporty/musical.
スポーツ／音楽が得意です／じゃありません。
supōtsu/ongaku ga tokui desu/ja arimasen.

I do/don't have a lot of spare time.
時間がたくさんあります／あまりありません。
jikan ga takusan arimasu/amari arimasen.

## VOCABULARY

| | | |
|---|---|---|
| spare time<br>余暇<br>yoka | hobby/pastime<br>趣味<br>shumi | to relax<br>くつろぐ<br>kutsurogu |
| activity<br>活動<br>katsudō | to be interested in<br>…に興味がある<br>...ni kyōmi ga aru | to enjoy<br>楽しむ<br>tanoshimu |

cooking
料理
ryōri

DIY
日曜大工
nichiyō-daiku

gaming
ゲーム
gēmu

gardening
ガーデニング
gādeningu

jogging
ジョギング
jogingu

listening to music
音楽を聞くこと
ongaku o kiku koto

reading
読書
dokusho

shopping
買物
kaimono

sports
スポーツ
supōtsu

travelling
旅行
ryokō

walking
散歩
sanpo

watching TV/films
テレビ／映画を見
ること
terebi/ēga o miru koto

Lively modern cities, ancient former capitals full of temples and shrines, mountains, coast, and islands – Japan has something for everyone.

## YOU MIGHT SAY...

How much is it to get in?
入場料はいくらですか。
nyūjōryō wa ikura desu ka?

Is there a discount for students/seniors?
学生／シニア割引はありますか。
gakusē/shinia waribiki wa arimasu ka?

Where is the tourist office?
観光案内所はどこですか。
kankō annaijo wa doko desu ka?

Are there sightseeing tours?
観光ツアーはありますか。
kankō tsuā wa arimasu ka?

Are there audio guides available?
音声ガイドはありますか。
onsē-gaido wa arimasu ka?

## YOU MIGHT HEAR...

Entry costs...
入場料は…円です。
nyūjōryō wa ...en desu.

There is/isn't a discount available.
割引があります／ありません。
waribiki ga arimasu/arimasen.

The tourist office is located...
観光案内所は…にあります。
kankō annaijo wa ...ni arimasu.

You can book a guided tour.
ガイドツアーの予約ができます。
gaido tsuā no yoyaku ga dekimasu.

Audio guides are/are not available.
音声ガイドがあります／ありません。
onsē-gaido ga arimasu/arimasen.

## VOCABULARY

| | | |
|---|---|---|
| tourist<br>観光客<br>kankōkyaku | excursion<br>小旅行<br>shōryokō | historic site<br>史跡<br>shiseki |
| tourist attraction<br>観光スポット<br>kankō supotto | holiday<br>休暇<br>kyūka | to visit<br>訪ねる<br>tazuneru |

## YOU SHOULD KNOW...

Some cultural and historical sites are closed on a Monday or Tuesday.

art gallery
美術館
bijutsukan

Buddhist temple
お寺
o-tera

castle
城
shiro

cathedral
大聖堂
daisēdō

city map
市内地図
shinai chizu

gardens
庭
niwa

guidebook
ガイドブック
gaido-bukku

museum
博物館
hakubutsukan

Shinto shrine
神社
jinja

sightseeing bus
観光バス
kankō basu

tour guide
観光ガイド
kankō gaido

tourist office
観光案内所
kankō annaijo

Japan offers a vast range of entertainment, from traditional Japanese theatre to animated films (アニメ anime) and cosplay.

### YOU MIGHT SAY...

What's on at the cinema/theatre?
映画館／劇場で何をやっていますか。
ēgakan/gekijō de nani o yatte imasu ka?

Do you want to go for a drink?
飲みに行きませんか。
nomi ni ikimasen ka?

Do you want to go and see a film/kabuki?
映画／歌舞伎を見に行きませんか。
ēga/kabuki o mi ni ikimasen ka?

Are there tickets for...?
…のチケットはありますか。
...no chiketto wa arimasu ka?

Two standard/first-class seats, please.
2等／1等席を2枚、お願いします。
nitō/ittō seki o ni-mai, onegai shimasu.

What time does it start?
何時に始まりますか。
nan-ji ni hajimarimasu ka?

### YOU MIGHT HEAR...

There's a film I'd like to see.
見たい映画があります。
mitai ēga ga arimasu.

You can buy tickets at a convenience store.
チケットはコンビニで買えますよ。
chiketto wa konbini de kaemasu yo.

There are no tickets left.
チケットは売り切れました。
chiketto wa urikiremashita.

It begins at 7 o'clock.
7時に始まります。
shichi-ji ni hajimarimasu.

Please turn off your mobile phones.
携帯の電源をお切りください。
kētai no dengen wa o-kiri kudasai.

| | | |
|---|---|---|
| drinks<br>飲み物<br>nomimono | festival<br>フェスティバル<br>fesutibaru | to see a show<br>ショーを見る<br>shō o miru |
| nightlife<br>ナイトライフ<br>naitoraifu | box office<br>切符売場<br>kippu uriba | to watch a film<br>映画を見る<br>ēga o miru |
| party<br>パーティー<br>pātii | to socialize<br>交流する<br>kōryū suru | to go dancing<br>踊りに行く<br>odori ni iku |
| show<br>ショー<br>shō | to order food/drinks<br>食べ物／飲みもの<br>を注文する<br>tabemono/nomimono o<br>chūmon suru | to enjoy oneself<br>楽しむ<br>tanoshimu |
| film<br>映画<br>ega | | |

## YOU SHOULD KNOW...

The iconic geisha seen in tourist performances and in the old areas of Kyoto are actually more likely to be apprentice geisha (舞子 maiko).

anime film
アニメ
anime

apprentice geisha
舞子
maiko

bar
バー
bā

bunraku puppet theatre
文楽
bunraku

cinema
映画館
ēgakan

comic storytelling
落語
rakugo

concert
コンサート
konsāto

cosplay
コスプレ
kosupure

festival
（お）祭り
(o-)matsuri

funfair
遊園地
yūenchi

kabuki
歌舞伎
kabuki

karaoke
カラオケ
karaoke

musical
ミュージカル
myūjikaru

Noh
能
nō

theatre
劇場
gekijō

Japan offers a wide choice of places to stay, from luxury Western-style hotels to minimalist capsule hotels. Japanese guest houses or B&Bs (民宿 minshuku) are a less expensive alternative to traditional inns (旅館 ryokan), and staying in a temple or shrine (宿坊 shukubō) is also popular. Self-catering options include short-term apartment lets in a ウィークリーマンション (wiikurii manshon), and communal living in cheaper hostels and guest houses for foreigners.

## YOU MIGHT SAY...

Have you got rooms available?
部屋はありますか。
heya wa arimasu ka?

How much is it per night?
一泊いくらですか。
ippaku ikura desu ka?

Is breakfast included?
朝ご飯付きですか。
asagohan-tsuki desu ka?

I'd like to check in/out, please.
チェックイン／チェックアウト
をお願いします。
chekku-in/chekku-auto o onegai shimasu.

What time do I have to check out?
チェックアウトは何時ですか。
chekku-auto wa nan-ji desu ka?

What time is breakfast served?
朝ご飯は何時ですか。
asagohan wa nan-ji desu ka?

I have a reservation.
予約してあります。
yoyaku shite arimasu.

I'd like to book a single/double room, please.
シングル／ダブルルームを予
約したいんですが。
shinguru/daburu rūmu o yoyaku shitai n desu ga.

Could I upgrade my room?
部屋をグレードアップできません
んか。
heya o gurēdoappu dekimasen ka?

I need fresh towels/more soap for my room.
新しいタオル／せっけんをお
願いします。
atarashii taoru/sekken o onegai shimasu.

I've lost my key.
鍵を失くしました。
kagi o nakushimashita.

Who do I make a complaint to?
苦情はどこに言ったらいいで
すか。
kujō wa doko ni ittara ii desu ka?

We have/don't have rooms available.
部屋があります／ありません。
heya ga arimasu/arimasen.

Our rates are...
料金は…円です。
ryōkin wa ...en desu.

Breakfast is/is not included.
朝食付きです／じゃありません。
chōshoku-tsuki desu/ja arimasen.

Breakfast is served at...
朝食は…時からです。
chōshoku wa ...ji kara desu.

May I have your room number, please?
お部屋番号をいただけますか。
o-heya bangō o itadakemasu ka?

May I see your documents, please?
書類を見せていただけますか。
shorui o misete itadakemasu ka?

You may check in after...
…時からチェックインできます。
...ji kara chekku-in dekimasu.

You must check out before...
…時までにチェックアウトしてください。
...made ni chekku-auto shite kudasai.

## VOCABULARY

bed and breakfast
朝食付き
chōshoku-tsuki

Japanese-style guesthouse
民宿
minshuku

short-term let
ウィークリーマンション
wiikurii manshon

full/half board
3/2食付き
san-/ni-shoku-tsuki

per person per night
1人1泊
hitori ippaku

receptionist
受付の人
uketsuke no hito

room service
ルームサービス
rūmu sābisu

wake-up call
モーニングコール
mōningu kōru

room number
部屋番号
heya bangō

"do not disturb" sign
「起こさないでください」の札
"okosanaide kudasai" no fuda

to check in/out
チェックイン／チェックアウトする
chekku-in/chekku-auto suru

to order room service
ルームサービスを頼む
rūmu sābisu o tanomu

capsule hotel
カプセルホテル
kapuseru hoteru

corridor
廊下
rōka

double room
ダブルルーム
daburu rūmu

hostel
ホステル
hosuteru

Japanese inn
旅館
ryokan

key card
カードキー
kādo kii

minibar
ミニバー
mini-bā

reception
受付
uketsuke

safe
金庫
kinko

single room
シングルルーム
shinguru rūmu

toiletries
化粧品
keshōhin

twin room
ツインルーム
tsuin rūmu

Visiting a hot spring (温泉 onsen), whether staying overnight or as a day trip, is a popular way to relax. Now that most homes have their own bathrooms, there are fewer traditional public bath houses that are not linked to hot springs, although new ones with extra facilities are appearing.

## YOU MIGHT SAY...

How much is admission?
入湯料はいくらですか。
nyūtōryō wa ikura desu ka?

I'd like to book the bath for private use.
貸切風呂を予約したいんですが。
kashikiri-buro o yoyaku shitai n desu ga.

Is the bath for men only/for women only/mixed?
お風呂は男性専用／女性専用／混浴ですか。
o-furo wa dansē-sen-yō/josē-sen-yō/kon'yoku desu ka?

Are towels provided?
タオルはついていますか。
taoru wa tsuite imasu ka?

Are there lockers?
ロッカーがありますか。
rokkā ga arimasu ka?

It's hot!
熱い!
atsui!

## YOU MIGHT HEAR...

Admission is ... yen.
入湯料は…です。
nyūtōryō wa ...en desu.

You can use the bath privately from ... to...
…から…まで貸切りで使えます。
...kara ...made kashikiri de tsukaemasu.

Please don't wear swimsuits.
水着を着ないでください。
mizugi o kinaide kudasai.

Please wash before entering the bath.
お風呂に入る前に体を洗ってください。
o-furo ni hairu mae ni karada o aratte kudasai.

Please don't put towels in the water.
タオルをお湯の中に入れないでください。
taoru o o-yu no naka ni irenaide kudasai.

## VOCABULARY

| | | |
|---|---|---|
| public bath house<br>銭湯<br>sentō | private use<br>貸切風呂<br>kashikiri-buro | changing area<br>脱衣場<br>datsuijo |
| men only<br>男性専用／男湯<br>dansē-sen-yō/otoko-yu | hot water<br>お湯<br>o-yu | locker<br>ロッカー<br>rokkā |
| women only<br>女性専用／女湯<br>josē-sen-yō/onna-yu | cold water<br>水<br>mizu | towel<br>タオル<br>taoru |
| mixed bathing<br>混浴<br>kon'yoku | indoor bath<br>内風呂<br>uchi-buro | washing bowl/bucket<br>洗面器<br>senmenki |

## YOU SHOULD KNOW...

Some places may still refuse entrance to people with tattoos, although attitudes are changing.

bath stool
風呂イス
furo-isu

cotton kimono
浴衣
yukata

entrance curtain
のれん
noren

footbath
足湯
ashi-yu

hot spring
温泉
onsen

outdoor bath
露天風呂
roten-buro

Camping is popular in Japan and campsites are generally well-equipped, some with pre-pitched tents or cabins. Booking is recommended at busy periods.

Have you got spaces available?
空きがありますか。
aki ga arimasu ka?

I'd like to book for ... nights.
…泊したいんですが。
...haku/paku shitai n desu ga.

How much is it per night?
一泊いくらですか。
ippaku ikura desu ka?

We have/don't have spaces available.
空きがあります／ありません。
aki ga arimasu/arimasen.

It costs ... per night.
1泊…円です。
ippaku ...en desu.

toilet/shower block
トイレ／シャワー施設
toire/shawā shisetsu

campsite
キャンプ場
kyanpujō

to camp
キャンプする
kyanpu suru

to pitch a tent
テントを張る
tento o haru

to take down a tent
テントをたたむ
tento o tatamu

sleeping bag
寝袋
nebukuro

tent
テント
tento

torch
懐中電灯
kaichū–dentō

Seaside activities are becoming increasingly popular, but primarily only during the summer months. In most areas, come the first of September, local authority lifeguards are no longer on duty, amenities are closed, and the beaches empty, whatever the weather.

## YOU MIGHT SAY...

Is swimming permitted here?
ここで泳いでもいいですか。
koko de oyoide mo ii desu ka?

Can we hire...?
…を借りられますか。
...o kariraremasu ka?

Can you surf here?
ここでサーフィンができますか。
koko de sāfin ga dekimasu ka?

Someone's drowning! Help!
人がおぼれています。助けてください！
hito ga oborete imasu. tasukete kudasai!

## YOU MIGHT HEAR...

Swimming is allowed/forbidden.
泳いでもいいです／水泳禁止です。
oyoide mo ii desu/suiē kinshi desu.

You can/can't surf here.
ここでサーフィンができます／できません。
koko de sāfin ga dekimasu/dekimasen.

There is no lifeguard on duty.
監視員はいません。
kanshi-in wa imasen.

It's too cold to swim today.
今日は泳ぐのには寒すぎます。
kyō wa oyogu no ni wa samusugimasu.

## VOCABULARY

"No swimming"
「 水泳禁止 」
"suiē kinshi"

bathing zone
水泳ゾーン
suiē zōn

suntan
日焼け
hiyake

sand
砂
suna

sea
海
umi

waves
波
nami

beach towel
ビーチタオル
biichi taoru

to sunbathe
日光浴する
nikkōyoku suru

to swim
泳ぐ
oyogu

beach ball
ビーチボール
biichi bōru

bikini
ビキニ
bikini

flip-flops
ビーチサンダル
biichi sandaru

lifeguard
監視員
kanshi-in

sunglasses
サングラス
sangurasu

sunhat
麦わら帽子
mugiwara-bōshi

sunscreen
日焼け止め
hiyakedome

swimsuit
水着
mizugi

swimming trunks
水泳パンツ
suiē pantsu

Western music is popular, while TV music shows are dominated by J-pop.

### YOU MIGHT SAY/HEAR...

I'm learning to play...
…を習っています。
...o naratte imasu.

My favourite group is...
好きなグループは…です。
suki-na gurūpu wa ...desu.

What kind of music do you like?
どんな音楽が好きですか。
donna ongaku ga suki desu ka?

### VOCABULARY

| | | |
|---|---|---|
| song 歌 uta | concert コンサート konsāto | Japanese folk music 民謡 min'yō |
| CD CD shii-dii | rock ロック rokku | to play an instrument 楽器を演奏する gakki o ensō suru |
| album アルバム arubamu | jazz ジャズ jazu | to sing 歌を歌う uta o utau |
| vinyl record アナログレコード anarogu rekōdo | J-pop J Pop jē-poppu | to listen to/stream music 音楽を聞く／ストリーミング ongaku o kiku/ sutoriimingu suru |
| band バンド bando | rap ラップ rappu | |
| live music ライブ音楽 raibu ongaku | classical クラシック kurashikku | to go to concerts コンサートに行く konsāto ni iku |

Bluetooth® speaker
ブルートゥーススピ
ーカー
burūtūsu supiikā

earphones
イヤホン
iyahon

headphones
ヘッドホン
heddohon

soundbar
サウンドバー
saundobā

speakers
スピーカー
supiikā

turntable
回転盤
kaitenban

**MUSICAL INSTRUMENTS**

accordion
アコーディオン
akōdion

acoustic guitar
アコースティックギ
ター
akōsutikku gitā

bass guitar
ベースギター
bēsu gitā

cello
チェロ
chero

clarinet
クラリネット
kurarinetto

double bass
ダブルベース
daburu bēsu

drum kit
ドラム
doramu

electric guitar
エレキギター
ereki gitā

flute
フルート
furūto

harp
ハープ
hāpu

keyboard
キーボード
kiibōdo

mouth organ
ハモニカ
hamonika

piano
ピアノ
piano

saxophone
サクソフォン
sakusofon

trombone
トロンボーン
toronbōn

trumpet
トランペット
toranpetto

tuba
チューバ
chūba

violin
バイオリン
baiorin

## TRADITIONAL JAPANESE INSTRUMENTS

hand drum
鼓
tsuzumi

Japanese drum
太鼓
taiko

Japanese flute
尺八
shakuhachi

Japanese lute
琵琶
biwa

koto
琴
koto

shamisen
三味線
shamisen

## GENERAL MUSIC

choir
合唱団
gasshōdan

conductor
指揮者
shikisha

musician
音楽家／ミュージシ
ャン
ongakuka/myūjishan

orchestra
オーケストラ
ōkesutora

sheet music
楽譜
gakufu

singer
歌手
kashu

### YOU MIGHT SAY...

Can I take photos here?
ここで写真を撮ってもいいで
すか。
koko de shashin o totte mo ii desu ka?

Could you take my/our picture,
please?
写真を撮ってもらえませんか。
shashin o totte moraemasen ka?

### YOU MIGHT HEAR...

Photography is/isn't allowed.
写真を撮ってもいいですよ／
撮影禁止です。
shashin o totte mo ii desu yo/satsuē-
kinshi desu.

Say cheese!
はい、チーズ！
hai, chiizu!

### VOCABULARY

| | | |
|---|---|---|
| photo 写真 shashin | drone ドローン dorōn | to take a photo/selfie 写真を撮る／自撮りする shashin o toru/jidori suru |
| selfie 自写 jisha | SD card SD カード esu-dii kādo | to upload a photo 写真をアップロードする shashin o appurōdo suru |
| selfie stick 自撮り棒 jidoribō | tripod 三脚 sankyaku | |

### YOU SHOULD KNOW...

The use of selfie sticks is banned in many places for safety reasons.

camera lens
カメラレンズ
kamera renzu

compact camera
コンパクトカメラ
konpakuto kamera

DSLR camera
デジタルカメラ／デ
ジカメ
dejitaru kamera/
dejikame

### YOU MIGHT SAY...

What would you like to play?
どんなゲームがしたいですか。
donna gēmu ga shitai desu ka?

What are the rules?
どんなルールですか。
donna rūru desu ka?

Shall we play a game?
ゲームをしませんか。
gēmu o shimasen ka?

### YOU MIGHT HEAR...

It's your turn.
…さんの番ですよ。
...san no ban desu yo.

Time's up!
時間切れです。
jikangire desu.

Shall we play something else?
他のゲームをしましょうか。
hoka no gēmu o shimashō ka?

### VOCABULARY

player
プレーヤー
purēyā

online game
オンラインゲーム
onrain gēmu

poker
ポーカー
pōkā

hand (in cards)
持ち札
mochi-fuda

to play
ゲームをする
gēmu o suru

to roll the dice
さいころを振る
saikoro o furu

to win
勝つ
katsu

to lose
負ける
makeru

cards
トランプ
toranpu

chess
チェス
chesu

counters
こま
koma

dice
さいころ
saikoro

game controller
ゲームコントローラ
gēmu kontorōrā

games console
ゲーム機
gēmu-ki

go
囲碁
igo

jigsaw puzzle
ジグゾーパズル
jiguzō pazuru

shogi
将棋
shōgi

sudoku
数独
sūdoku

video game
ビデオゲーム
bideo gēmu

virtual reality headset
VR ヘッドセット
bui-āru heddosetto

While Western crafts have gained popularity, Japan's traditional arts and crafts are also still practised.

## VOCABULARY

| | | |
|---|---|---|
| handicrafts<br>手工芸<br>shukōgē | to paint<br>絵を描く<br>e o kaku | to sew<br>縫う<br>nuu |
| amateur<br>アマチュア<br>amachua | to sketch<br>スケッチする<br>suketchi suru | to knit<br>編み物をする<br>amimono o suru |

## GENERAL

ball of wool
毛糸(玉)
kēto(dama)

buttons
ボタン
botan

crochet hook
かぎ針
kagibari

fabric
布
nuno

fabric scissors
裁縫ばさみ
saihō-basami

knitting needles
編み針
amibari

needle and thread
針と糸
hari to ito

oil paint
油絵具
abura enogu

pins
待ち針
machibari

safety pin
安全ピン
anzen pin

sewing box
裁縫箱
saihō bako

sewing machine
ミシン
mishin

sketchpad
スケッチブック
suketchi bukku

tape measure
メジャー
mejā

watercolours
水彩絵具
suisai enogu

## CRAFTS

embroidery
刺繍
shishū

model-making
模型作り
mokē-zukuri

pottery
陶芸
tōgē

bonsai
盆栽
bonsai

calligraphy
書道
shodō

calligraphy brush,
inkstick, inkstone
筆, 墨, 硯
fude, sumi, suzuri

flower arranging
生け花
ikebana

flowers
花
hana

ink painting
墨絵
sumi-e

Japanese cake
和菓子
wagashi

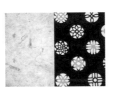

Japanese paper
和紙
washi

matcha green tea
抹茶
matcha

origami
折り紙
origami

tea bowl
茶碗
chawan

tea ceremony
茶の湯／茶道
chanoyu/sadō

There are opportunities to watch or take part in all kinds of sports in Japan, from traditional martial arts to team games and winter sports. While in Japan, you may wish to participate in a sport or head to the gym, or you may simply want to chat about the latest baseball or football results.

football pitch
サッカーフィールド
sakkā fiirudo

centre circle
センターサークル
sentā sākuru

penalty box
ペナルティーボックス
penarutii bokkusu

goal
ゴール
gōru

**YOU MIGHT SAY...**

I like playing sports.
スポーツをするのが好きです。
supōtsu o suru no ga suki desu.

Where is the nearest...?
一番近い…はどこですか。
ichiban chikai ...wa doko desu ka?

I don't like sports very much.
スポーツがあまり好きじゃありません。
supōtsu ga amari suki ja arimasen.

I play football/tennis.
サッカー／テニスをします。
sakkā/tenisu o shimasu.

I'd like to book...
…の予約がしたいんですが。
...no yoyaku ga shitai n desu ga.

**YOU MIGHT HEAR...**

There's a ... nearby.
近くに…があります。
chikaku ni ...ga arimasu.

Do you do any sports?
何かスポーツをしますか。
nanika supōtsu o shimasu ka?

Do you follow any sports?
どんなスポーツのファンですか。
donna supōtsu no fan desu ka?

What's your favourite team?
好きなチームは何ですか。
suki-na chiimu wa nan desu ka?

Who's your favourite player?
好きな選手は誰ですか。
suki-na senshu wa dare desu ka?

**VOCABULARY**

| | | |
|---|---|---|
| tournament<br>トーナメント<br>tōnamento | sportsperson<br>スポーツをする人<br>supōtsu o suru hito | teammate<br>チームメート<br>chiimumēto |
| competition<br>競技会／大会<br>kyōgikai/taikai | champion<br>チャンピオン<br>chanpion | coach<br>コーチ<br>kōchi |
| league<br>リーグ<br>riigu | competitor<br>出場選手／競技相手<br>shutsujō senshu/kyōgi aite | manager<br>マネージャー<br>manējā |

| official | points | to win |
|---|---|---|
| 競技役員 | 得点 | 勝つ |
| kyōgi yakuin | tokuten | katsu |

| spectators | to compete | to lose |
|---|---|---|
| 観客 | 競争する | 負ける |
| kankyaku | kyōsō suru | makeru |

| match | to score | to draw |
|---|---|---|
| 試合 | 得点する | 引き分ける |
| shiai | tokuten suru | hikiwakeru |

leisure centre
レジャーセンター
rejā sentā

medal
メダル
medaru

podium
表彰台
hyōshōdai

referee
レフェリー
referii

scoreboard
スコアボード
sukoabōdo

stadium
スタジアム
sutajiamu

stands
観覧席
kanranseki

team
チーム
chiimu

trophy
トロフィー
torofii

Gyms in Japan may not have the same range of facilities and equipment as UK ones. Jogging is popular, and the route around the Imperial Palace in Tokyo is particularly well known.

### YOU MIGHT SAY...

I'd like to join the gym.
ジムに入会したいです。
jimu ni nyūkai shitai desu.

I'd like to book a class.
クラスの予約がしたいです。
kurasu no yoyaku ga shitai desu.

What classes can you do here?
ここにはどんなクラスがありますか。
koko ni wa donna kurasu ga arimasu ka?

### YOU MIGHT HEAR...

Would you like to book a personal trainer?
パーソナルトレーナーの予約をなさいますか。
pāsonaru torēnā no yoyaku o nasaimasu ka?

What time would you like to book for?
何時に予約なさいますか。
nan-ji ni yoyaku nasaimasu ka?

### VOCABULARY

| | | |
|---|---|---|
| gym ジム jimu | fitness class フィットネスクラブ fittonesu kurabu | running ランニング ranningu |
| gym instructor インストラクター insutorakutā | Pilates ピラテス piratesu | to exercise 運動する undō suru |
| gym membership ジム会員 jimu kai-in | yoga ヨガ yoga | to go for a run 走りに行く hashiri ni iku |
| personal trainer パーソナルトレーナー pāsonaru torēnā | sit-ups 腹筋運動 fukkin undō | to go to the gym ジムに行く jimu ni iku |
| | press-ups 腕立て伏せ udetatefuse | to book a class クラスを予約する kurasu o yoyaku suru |

changing room
着替え室
kigae-shitsu

cross trainer
クロストレーナー
kurosu torēnā

dumbbell
ダンベル
danberu

exercise bike
エアロバイク
earobaiku

gym ball
ジムボール
jimu bōru

kettle bell
ケトルベル
ketoruberu

locker
ロッカー
rokkā

rowing machine
ローイングマシーン
rōingu mashiin

showers
シャワー
shawā

skipping rope
縄跳び
nawatobi

treadmill
ランニングマシーン
ranningu mashiin

weightlifting bench
ベンチプレス
benchi puresu

Baseball is a major sport in Japan, and the annual summer high school tournament at Kōshien Stadium draws a vast TV audience.

## VOCABULARY

| | | |
|---|---|---|
| baseball stadium<br>野球場<br>yakyū-jō | home plate<br>本塁<br>honrui | mound<br>マウンド<br>maundo |
| batter<br>バッター<br>battā | home run<br>ホームラン<br>hōmuran | pitcher<br>ピッチャー<br>pitchā |
| catcher<br>キャッチャー<br>kyatchā | inning<br>回<br>kai | softball<br>ソフトボール<br>sofutobōru |

baseball
野球のボール
yakyū no bōru

baseball bat
バット
batto

baseball cap
野球帽
yakyūbō

baseball game
野球
yakyū

baseball mitt
グローブ
gurōbu

baseball player
野球選手
yakyū senshu

Basketball has become popular among younger Japanese people, with success in the Asian Games. Some professional teams now play in the B. League.

## VOCABULARY

wheelchair basketball
車椅子バスケットボール
kurumaisu
basukettobōru

slam dunk
スラムダンク
suramu danku

free throw
フリースロー
furii surō

to play basketball
バスケットをする
basuketto o suru

to catch
ボールを受け取る
bōru o uketoru

to throw
投げる
nageru

to dribble
ドリブルする
doriburu suru

to block
ブロックする
burokku suru

to mark
…をマークする
…o māku suru

basket
バスケット
basuketto

basketball
バスケットのボール
basuketto no bōru

basketball court
コート
kōto

basketball game
バスケット(ボール)
basuketto(bōru)

basketball player
バスケット選手
basuketto senshu

basketball shoes
バスケットシューズ
basuketto shūzu

Football is now the most popular sport among young Japanese people, thanks partly to the 2002 World Cup being held jointly in Japan and South Korea.

## YOU MIGHT SAY...

Are you going to watch the match?
試合を見ますか。
shiai o mimasu ka?

What's the score?
得点は何点ですか。
tokuten wa nan-ten desu ka?

## YOU MIGHT HEAR...

The score is...
得点は…です。
tokuten wa ...desu.

Go on!
がんばれ!
ganbare!

## VOCABULARY

defender
ディフェンダー
difendā

striker
ストライカー
sutoraikā

substitute
補欠
hoketsu

kick-off
キックオフ
kikku-ofu

half-time
ハーフタイム
hāfu-taimu

full-time
試合時間
shiai jikan

additional time
アディショナルタイム
adishonaru taimu

free kick
フリーキック
furii kikku

header
ヘディング
hedingu

foul
ファウル
fauru

offside
オフサイド
ofusaido

penalty
ペナルティー
penarutii

penalty box
ペナルティーボックス
penarutii bokkusu

to play football
サッカーをする
sakkā o suru

to kick
ける
keru

to shoot
シュートする
shūto suru

to pass the ball
ボールをパスする
bōru o pasu suru

to score a goal
ゴールを決める
gōru o kimeru

assistant referee
線審
senshin

football
サッカーボール
sakkā bōru

football boots
サッカーシューズ
sakkā shūzu

football match
サッカー
sakkā

football pitch
サッカーフィールド
sakkā fiirudo

football player
サッカー選手
sakkā senshu

goal
ゴール
gōru

goalkeeper
ゴールキーパー
gōrukiipā

goalkeeper's gloves
キーパーグローブ
kiipā gurōbu

shin pads
すね当て
suneate

whistle
ホイッスル
hoissuru

yellow/red card
イエロー/レッドカード
ierō/reddo kādo

## VOCABULARY

forward
フォワード
fowādo

back
バックス
bakkusu

try
トライ
torai

conversion
コンバージョン
konbājon

penalty kick
ペナルティーキック
penarutii kikku

drop goal
ドロップゴール
doroppu gōru

tackle
タックル
takkuru

pass
パス
pasu

mouthguard
マウスピース
mausupiisu

to play rugby
ラグビーをする
ragubii o suru

to tackle
タックルする
takkuru suru

to score a try
トライを決める
torai o kimeru

goalposts
ゴールポスト
gōruposuto

rugby
ラグビー
ragubii

rugby ball
ラグビーボール
ragubii bōru

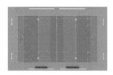

rugby field
ラグビー場
ragubii-jō

rugby player
ラグビー選手
ragubii senshu

scrum
スクラム
sukuramu

## YOU MIGHT SAY...

I'm not a strong swimmer.
泳ぐのが上手じゃありません。
oyogu no ga jōzu ja arimasen.

Can I hire...?
…が借りられますか。
...ga kariraremasu ka?

## YOU MIGHT HEAR...

You can hire...
…が借りられます。
...ga kariraremasu.

You must wear a lifejacket.
救命胴衣をつけなければいけません。
kyūmēdōi o tsukenakereba ikemasen.

## VOCABULARY

| | | |
|---|---|---|
| swimming 水泳 suiē | length 長さ nagasa | to swim 泳ぐ oyogu |
| breaststroke 平泳ぎ hiraoyogi | swimming lesson 水泳教室 suiē kyōshitsu | to dive 潜る moguru |
| backstroke 背泳ぎ seoyogi | diving ダイビング daibingu | to surf サーフィンをする sāfin o suru |
| front crawl クロール kurōru | angling 魚釣り sakana tsuri | to paddle こいで進む koide susumu |
| butterfly バタフライ batafurai | angler 釣り人 tsuribito | to row ボートをこぐ bōto o kogu |
| lane レーン rēn | sailor 船員 sen'in | to sail 帆走する hansō suru |
| deep/shallow 深い／浅い fukai/asai | surfer サーファー sāfā | to fish 釣りをする tsuri o suru |

187

armbands
アームバンド
āmubando

diver
ダイバー
daibā

diving board
飛込み台
tobikomidai

goggles
ゴーグル
gōguru

swimmer
水泳する人
suiē suru hito

swimming cap
水泳帽
suiēbō

swimming pool
プール
pūru

swimming trunks
海水パンツ
kaisui pantsu

swimsuit
水着
mizugi

**OPEN WATER**

canoeing
カヌーに乗ること
kanū ni noru koto

jet ski
ジェットスキー
jetto sukii

kayaking
カヤックに乗ること
kayakku ni noru koto

lifejacket
救命胴衣
kyūmēdōi

oars
オール
ōru

paddle
パドル
padoru

paddleboarding
パドルボード
padorubōdo

sailing boat
帆船
hansen

scuba diving
スキューバダイビング
sukyūba daibingu

snorkelling
シュノーケリング
shunōkeringu

surfboard
サーフボード
sāfubōdo

surfing
サーフィン
sāfin

waterskiing
ウォータースキー
wōtāsukii

wetsuit
ウェットスーツ
wettosūtsu

windsurfing
ウィンドサーフィン
windosāfin

Public tennis courts can be found in some big city parks, but they are popular and often need to be booked well in advance. Courts at private clubs and some big hotels are more expensive. Badminton is now gaining popularity among younger Japanese.

## VOCABULARY

| | | |
|---|---|---|
| net<br>ネット<br>netto | fault<br>フォールト<br>fōruto | to play tennis<br>テニスをする<br>tenisu o suru |
| ace<br>サービスエース<br>sābisu ēsu | rally<br>ラリー<br>rarii | to play badminton<br>バドミントンをする<br>badominton o suru |
| serve<br>サーブ<br>sābu | game, set and match<br>ゲーム、セット、マッチ<br>gēmu, setto, matchi | to hit<br>打つ<br>utsu |
| backhand<br>バックハンド<br>bakkuhando | singles<br>シングルス<br>shingurusu | to serve<br>サーブする<br>sābu suru |
| forehand<br>フォアハンド<br>foahando | doubles<br>ダブルス<br>daburusu | to break someone's serve<br>サーブを破る<br>sābu o yaburu |

## BADMINTON

badminton
バドミントン
badominton

badminton racket
バドミントンラケット
badominton raketto

shuttlecock
シャトル
shatoru

## SQUASH

squash
スカッシュ
sukasshu

squash ball
スカッシュボール
sukasshu bōru

squash racket
スカッシュラケット
sukasshu raketto

## TENNIS

ball boy/girl
ボールボーイ／ガ
ール
bōru bōi/gāru

line judge
線審
senshin

tennis
テニス
tenisu

tennis ball
テニスのボール
tenisu no bōru

tennis court
テニスコート
tenisu kōto

tennis player
テニス選手
tenisu senshu

tennis racket
テニスラケット
tenisu raketto

umpire
主審
shushin

umpire's chair
審判台
shinpandai

Japan's many mountainous areas lend themselves to skiing and other winter sports, particularly in the Japan Alps and Hokkaido.

### YOU MIGHT SAY...

Can I hire some skis?
スキーを借りられますか。
sukii o kariraremasu ka?

I'd like a skiing lesson, please.
スキーレッスンを受けたいんですが。
sukii ressun o uketai n desu ga.

I can't ski very well.
スキーがあまり上手じゃありません。
sukii ga amari jōzu ja arimasen.

What are the snow conditions like?
雪の状態はどうですか。
yuki no jōtai wa dō desu ka?

I've hurt myself.
けがをしました。
kega o shimashita.

### YOU MIGHT HEAR...

You can hire skis here.
ここでスキーが借りられます。
koko de sukii ga kariraremasu.

You can book a skiing lesson here.
ここでスキーレッスンを申し込めます。
koko de sukii ressun o mōshikomemasu.

Do you have skiing experience?
スキーの経験がありますか。
sukii no kēken ga arimasu ka?

The piste is open/closed today.
今日、ピストはオープンして／閉まっています。
kyō, pisuto wa ōpun shite/shimatte imasu.

There's an avalanche risk.
雪崩の恐れがあります。
nadare no osore ga arimasu.

### VOCABULARY

skier
スキーヤー
sukiiyā

ski instructor
スキー指導員
sukii shidōin

ski patrol
スキーパトロール
sukii patorōru

ski resort
スキー場
sukii-jō

ski lift
スキーリフト
sukii rifuto

piste
ピスト
pisuto

snow
雪
yuki

avalanche
なだれ
nadare

to ski (off-piste)
スキーをする
sukii o suru

ice
氷
kōri

to skate
スケートをする
sukēto o suru

to snowboard
スノーボードをする
sunōbōdo o suru

ice skates
スケート靴
sukēto-gutsu

ice skating
アイススケート
aisu sukēto

ski boots
スキーブーツ
sukii būtsu

ski goggles
スキーゴーグル
sukii gōguru

ski helmet
スキーヘルメット
sukii herumetto

ski jacket
スキージャケット
sukii jaketto

ski poles
ストック
sutokku

skis
スキー板
sukii ita

snowboard
スノーボード
sunōbōdo

Walking, hiking, and climbing are becoming increasingly popular in Japan, with numerous mountain huts open in the summer months.

## VOCABULARY

| | | |
|---|---|---|
| first-aid kit<br>救急箱<br>kyūkyūbako | hiking trail<br>ハイキングコース<br>haikingu kōsu | waterproof jacket<br>防水ジャケット<br>bōsui-jaketto |
| GPS<br>GPS<br>jii-pii-esu | path<br>小道<br>komichi | to go hiking<br>ハイキングをする<br>haikingu o suru |
| mountain rescue<br>service<br>山岳救助隊<br>sangaku kyūjotai | summit<br>頂上<br>chōjō | to go climbing<br>登山する<br>tozan suru |

compass
コンパス
konpasu

crampons
アイゼン
aizen

ice axe
ピッケル
pikkeru

rope
ロープ
rōpu

walking boots
トレッキングシューズ
torekkingu shūzu

walking poles
トレッキングポール
torekkingu pōru

Japan's golf courses and golf clubs were known for being extremely expensive and exclusive in the past, but now many courses have become more accessible to the public. Multi-storey driving ranges are common in cities.

## VOCABULARY

| | | |
|---|---|---|
| golfer<br>ゴルファー<br>gorufā | green<br>グリーン<br>guriin | hole<br>ホール<br>hōru |
| caddie<br>キャディー<br>kyadii | clubhouse<br>クラブハウス<br>kurabuhausu | hole-in-one<br>ホールインワン<br>hōru-in-wan |
| golf course<br>ゴルフコース<br>gorufu kōsu | bunker<br>バンカー<br>bankā | to play golf<br>ゴルフをする<br>gorufu o suru |

driving range
ゴルフ練習場
gorufu renshū-jō

golf bag
ゴルフバッグ
gorufu baggu

golf ball
ゴルフボール
gorufu bōru

golf buggy
ゴルフカート
gorufu kāto

golf club
ゴルフクラブ
gorufu kurabu

tee
ティー
tii

Japan has a long history of martial arts, including archery and kendo (sparring with bamboo swords) as well as the better-known judo and karate. The national sport of sumo has many rituals linked to Shinto practices.

## VOCABULARY

| | | |
|---|---|---|
| dojo<br>道場<br>dōjō | punch<br>パンチ<br>panchi | to wrestle<br>格闘する<br>kakutō suru |
| instructor<br>先生<br>sensē | throw<br>投げ<br>nage | to punch<br>なぐる<br>naguru |
| player<br>競技者<br>kyōgisha | knockout<br>ノックアウト<br>nokkuauto | to throw<br>…を投げる<br>…o nageru |
| opponent<br>相手<br>aite | bow<br>弓<br>yumi | to kick<br>ける<br>keru |
| match<br>試合<br>shiai | arrow<br>矢<br>ya | to strike<br>打つ<br>utsu |

## MARTIAL ARTS AND COMBAT SPORTS

aikido
合気道
aikidō

bamboo sword
竹刀
shinai

boxing
ボクシング
bokushingu

Japanese archery
弓道
kyūdō

judo
柔道
jūdō

karate
空手
karate

kendo
剣道
kendo

taekwondo
テコンドー
tekondō

wrestling
レスリング
resuringu

## SUMO

sumo referee
行司
gyōji

sumo wrestler
相撲取り
sumō-tori

loincloth
まわし
mawashi

sumo ring
土俵
dohyō

### VOCABULARY

runner
走者
sōsha

race
レース
rēsu

marathon
マラソン
marason

sprint
短距離走
tankyorisō

relay
リレー
rirē

lane
レーン
rēn

start/finish line
スタート／ゴールライン
sutāto/gōru rain

heat
予選
yosen

final
決勝戦
kesshōsen

triple jump
3段飛び
sandan-tobi

heptathlon
ヘプタスロン
heputasuron

decathlon
デカスロン
dekasuron

starter's gun
スターターピストル
sutātā pisutoru

to do athletics
陸上競技をする
rikujō kyōgi o suru

to run
走る
hashiru

to race
競走する
kyōsō suru

to jump
跳ぶ
tobu

to throw
投げる
nageru

athlete
陸上競技の選手
rikujō kyōgi no senshu

discus
円盤投げ
enban-nage

high jump
走り高跳び
hashiri takatobi

hurdles
ハードル
hādoru

javelin
やり投げ
yari-nage

long jump
走り幅跳び
hashiri-habatobi

pole vault
棒高跳び
bō-takatobi

running track
トラック
torakku

shot put
砲丸投げ
hōgan-nage

stopwatch
ストップウォッチ
sutoppu wotchi

spikes
スパイク
supaiku

starting blocks
スターティングブロ
ック
sutātingu burokku

199

American football
アメフト
amefuto

cricket
クリケット
kuriketto

curling
カーリング
kāringu

gateball
ゲートボール
gētobōru

gymnastics
体操
taisō

horse racing
競馬
kēba

ice hockey
アイスホッケー
aisu hokkē

keirin
競輪
kērin

motor racing
カーレース
kā rēsu

skateboarding
スケートボード
sukētobōdo

table tennis
卓球
takkyū

volleyball
バレーボール
barēbōru

# HEALTH | 健康

If you are a short-term visitor or student in Japan, make sure that you have adequate health cover in your travel insurance. People staying in Japan for more than three months must have health insurance, either through their employer or through the national public health insurance scheme. A health insurance card must be shown when seeking a consultation or treatment.

first aid kit
救急箱
kyūkyūbako

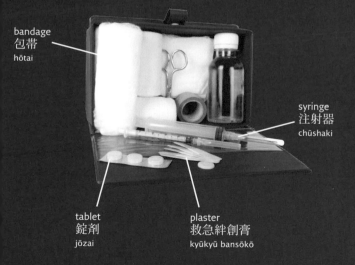

bandage
包帯
hōtai

syringe
注射器
chūshaki

tablet
錠剤
jōzai

plaster
救急絆創膏
kyūkyū bansōkō

The pharmacy is usually the first port of call for most minor ailments, especially since smaller villages may not be served by a clinic.

### YOU MIGHT SAY...

I don't feel well.
気分がよくないです。
kibun ga yokunai desu.

I've been feeling unwell.
ずっと気分が悪いです。
zutto kibun ga warui desu.

I've hurt my...
…を痛めました。
...o itamemashita.

I'm going to be sick.
吐きそうです。
haki-sō desu.

I need to see a doctor.
お医者さんに診てもらう必要があります。
o-isha-san ni mite morau hitsuyō ga arimasu.

I need to go to hospital.
病院に行く必要があります。
byōin ni iku hitsuyō ga arimasu.

Call an ambulance.
救急車を呼んでください。
kyūkyūsha o yonde kudasai.

### YOU MIGHT HEAR...

What's wrong?
どうしましたか。
dō shimashita ka?

Where does it hurt?
どこが痛みますか。
doko ga itamimasu ka?

### VOCABULARY

specialist
専門医
senmon'i

patient
患者
kanja

illness
病気
byōki

first aid
応急手当
ōkyū teate

pain
痛み
itami

mental health
精神衛生
sēshin ēsē

| treatment | health insurance card | to recover |
|---|---|---|
| 治療 | 健康保険証 | 回復する |
| chiryō | kenkō hoken-shō | kaifuku suru |

| recovery | healthy | to look after |
|---|---|---|
| 回復 | 健康的な | 面倒を見る |
| kaifuku | kenkōteki-na | mendō o miru |

| health insurance | to be unwell | to treat |
|---|---|---|
| 健康保険 | 元気じゃない | 治療する |
| kenkō hoken | genki ja nai | chiryō suru |

**YOU SHOULD KNOW...**

The national health insurance scheme covers 70% of any costs, with the remainder paid by the individual.

doctor
医者／お医者さん
isha/o-isha-san

hospital
病院
byōin

nurse
看護師
kangoshi

paramedic
救急救命士
kyūkyū kyūmēshi

pharmacist
薬剤師
yakuzaishi

pharmacy
薬局／薬屋
kusuri-ya/yakkyoku

In Japanese, possessive adjectives (for example, *my*, *his*, *their*) are not used to refer to body parts; the context makes it clear to whom they belong.

## VOCABULARY

| | | |
|---|---|---|
| throat<br>のど<br>nodo | tongue<br>舌<br>shita | sense of taste<br>味覚<br>mikaku |
| genitals<br>性器<br>sēki | skin<br>皮膚<br>hifu | sense of touch<br>触覚<br>shokkaku |
| breast<br>乳房<br>chibusa | (body) hair<br>髪<br>kami | to see<br>見る<br>miru |
| eyelash<br>まつ毛<br>matsuge | height<br>身長<br>shinchō | to smell<br>においをかぐ<br>nioi o kagu |
| eyebrow<br>眉毛<br>mayuge | weight<br>体重<br>taijū | to hear<br>聞く<br>kiku |
| eyelid<br>まぶた<br>mabuta | sense of hearing<br>聴覚<br>chōkaku | to touch<br>触る<br>sawaru |
| nostrils<br>鼻の孔<br>hana no ana | sense of sight<br>視覚<br>shikaku | to taste<br>味わう<br>ajiwau |
| lips<br>唇<br>kuchibiru | sense of smell<br>嗅覚<br>kyūkaku | to lose one's balance<br>バランスを失う<br>baransu o ushinau |

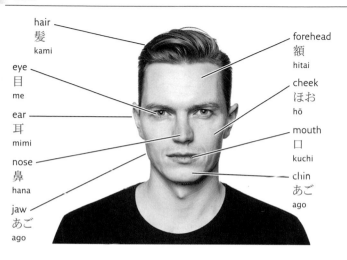

hair
髪
kami

forehead
額
hitai

eye
目
me

cheek
ほお
hō

ear
耳
mimi

mouth
口
kuchi

nose
鼻
hana

chin
あご
ago

jaw
あご
ago

## HAND

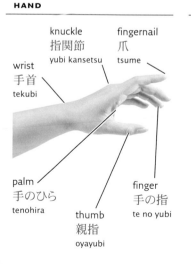

knuckle
指関節
yubi kansetsu

fingernail
爪
tsume

wrist
手首
tekubi

palm
手のひら
tenohira

thumb
親指
oyayubi

finger
手の指
te no yubi

## FOOT

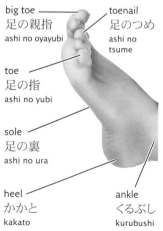

big toe
足の親指
ashi no oyayubi

toenail
足のつめ
ashi no tsume

toe
足の指
ashi no yubi

sole
足の裏
ashi no ura

heel
かかと
kakato

ankle
くるぶし
kurubushi

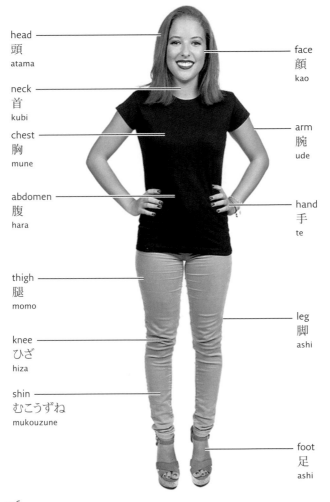

head
頭
atama

face
顔
kao

neck
首
kubi

chest
胸
mune

arm
腕
ude

abdomen
腹
hara

hand
手
te

thigh
腿
momo

leg
脚
ashi

knee
ひざ
hiza

shin
むこうずね
mukouzune

foot
足
ashi

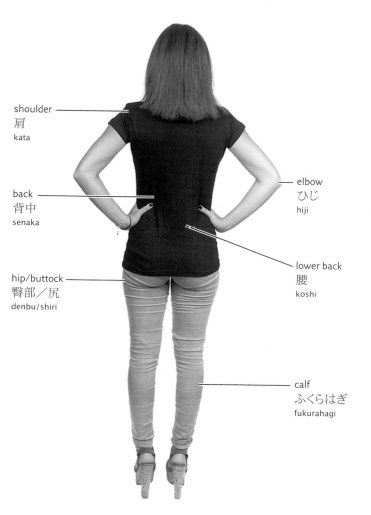

shoulder
肩
kata

back
背中
senaka

hip/buttock
臀部／尻
denbu/shiri

elbow
ひじ
hiji

lower back
腰
koshi

calf
ふくらはぎ
fukurahagi

Hopefully this is not vocabulary you will need very often, but it is useful to have the necessary terminology at your disposal, should the need arise.

### VOCABULARY

| | | |
|---|---|---|
| skeleton<br>骨格<br>kokkaku | kidney<br>腎臓<br>jinzō | bone<br>骨<br>hone |
| organ<br>臓器<br>zōki | intestines<br>腸<br>chō | muscle<br>筋肉<br>kinniku |
| brain<br>脳<br>nō | digestive system<br>消化器官<br>shōka kikan | tendon<br>腱<br>ken |
| heart<br>心臓<br>shinzō | bladder<br>膀胱<br>bōkō | tissue<br>組織<br>soshiki |
| lung<br>肺<br>hai | blood<br>血液／血<br>ketsueki/chi | cell<br>細胞<br>saibō |
| liver<br>肝臓<br>kanzō | oxygen<br>酸素<br>sanso | artery<br>動脈<br>dōmyaku |
| stomach<br>胃<br>i | joint<br>関節<br>kansetsu | vein<br>静脈<br>jōmyaku |

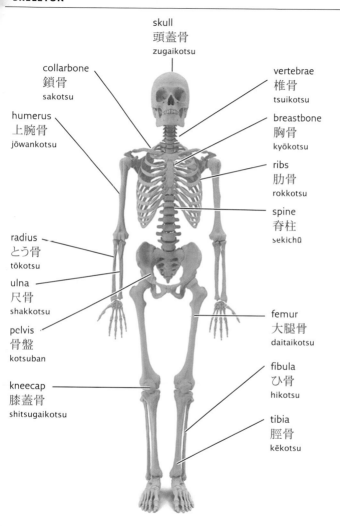

skull
頭蓋骨
zugaikotsu

collarbone
鎖骨
sakotsu

vertebrae
椎骨
tsuikotsu

humerus
上腕骨
jōwankotsu

breastbone
胸骨
kyōkotsu

ribs
肋骨
rokkotsu

spine
脊柱
sekichū

radius
とう骨
tōkotsu

ulna
尺骨
shakkotsu

pelvis
骨盤
kotsuban

femur
大腿骨
daitaikotsu

fibula
ひ骨
hikotsu

kneecap
膝蓋骨
shitsugaikotsu

tibia
脛骨
kēkotsu

There is no equivalent of the GP practice in Japan. Instead, patients can seek treatment at their chosen private or public clinic or hospital. Apart from large general hospitals, each smaller hospital or clinic has its own specialisms.

**YOU MIGHT SAY...**

I'd like to make an appointment.
予約したいんですが。
yoyaku shitai n desu ga.

I have an appointment with Dr...
…先生に予約してあります。
...sensē ni yoyaku shite arimasu.

I'm allergic to...
…にアレルギーがあります。
...ni arerugii ga arimasu.

I take medication for...
…の薬を飲んでいます。
...no kusuri o nonde imasu.

**YOU MIGHT HEAR...**

Your appointment is at ... o'clock.
予約は…時です。
yoyaku wa ...ji desu.

The doctor/nurse will call you through.
医師／看護師がお呼びします。
ishi/kangoshi ga o-yobi shimasu.

What are your symptoms?
どんな症状ですか。
donna shōjō desu ka?

May I examine you?
診てみましょうか。
mite mimashō ka?

Tell me if that hurts.
痛かったら言ってください。
itakattara itte kudasai.

Do you have any allergies?
何かアレルギーがありますか。
nanika arerugii ga arimasu ka?

Do you take any medication?
何か治療のために薬を飲んでいますか。
nanika chiryō no tame ni kusuri o nonde imasu ka?

Take two tablets twice a day.
1日に2回、2錠ずつ飲んでください。
ichi-nichi ni ni-kai, ni-jō zutsu nonde kudasai.

You need to see a specialist.
専門医に診てもらってください。
senmon'i ni mite moratte kudasai.

appointment
予約
yoyaku

antibiotics
抗生物質
kōsēbusshitsu

vaccination
予防接種
yobōsesshu

clinic
診療所
shinryōjo

the pill
ピル
piru

injection
注射
chūsha

examination room
診察室
shinsatsu-shitsu

sleeping pill
睡眠薬
suimin'yaku

to examine
診察する
shinsatsu suru

examination
診察
shinsatsu

prescription
処方せん
shohōsen

to be on medication
薬物治療を受けて
いる
yakubutsu chiryō o ukete iru

test
検査
kensa

home visit
往診
ōshin

blood pressure monitor
血圧計
ketsuatsukē

examination table
診察台
shinsatsudai

stethoscope
聴診器
chōshinki

syringe
注射器
chūshaki

thermometer
体温計
taionkē

waiting room
待合室
machiai-shitsu

## YOU MIGHT SAY...

Can I book an emergency appointment?
救急の予約がしたいんですが。
kyūkyū no yoyaku ga shitai n desu ga.

I have toothache.
歯が痛いです。
ha ga itai desu.

I have an abscess.
うんでいます。
unde imasu.

My filling has come out.
詰め物が取れました。
tsumemono ga toremashita.

I've broken my tooth.
歯が折れました。
ha ga oremashita.

My dentures are broken.
入れ歯が壊れました。
ireba ga kowaremashita.

## YOU MIGHT HEAR...

We don't have any emergency appointments available.
救急の予約はできません。
kyūkyū no yoyaku wa dekimasen.

Your tooth has to come out.
歯を抜かなければいけませんね。
ha o nukanakereba ikemasen ne.

You need a new filling.
新しい詰め物をしなければいけませんね。
atarashii tsumemono o shinakereba ikemasen ne.

## VOCABULARY

check-up
定期健診
tēki kenshin

molar
臼歯
kyūshi

incisor
切歯
sesshi

canine
犬歯
kenshi

wisdom teeth
親知らず
oyashirazu

filling
詰め物
tsumemono

crown
歯冠
shikan

toothache
歯痛
shitsū

extraction
抜歯
basshi

root canal treatment
根管治療
konkan chiryō

abscess
腫れ
hare

to brush one's teeth
歯を磨く
ha o migaku

braces
歯列矯正器
shiretsukōsēki

dental floss
デンタルフロス
dentaru-furosu

dental nurse
歯科助手
shika joshu

dentist
歯医者／歯科医
haisha/shika-i

dentist's chair
歯医者の椅子
haisha no isu

dentist's drill
歯科用ドリル
shikayō doriru

dentures
入れ歯
ireba

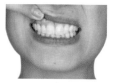

gums
歯茎
haguki

teeth
歯
ha

In Japan, both ophthalmologists and opticians carry out eye tests, and opticians supply glasses and contact lenses. Japan is known for manufacturing high-quality lenses.

### YOU MIGHT SAY...

Can I book an appointment?
予約したいんですが。
yoyaku shitai n desu ga.

Do you repair glasses?
眼鏡を直してもらえますか。
megane o naoshite moraemasu ka?

### YOU MIGHT HEAR...

Your appointment is at ... o'clock.
予約は…時です。
yoyaku wa …ji desu.

Look up/down/ahead.
上／下／前を見てください。
ue/shita/mae o mite kudasai.

### VOCABULARY

ophthalmologist
眼科医／眼医者
ganka-i/me-isha

reading glasses
読書用メガネ
dokusho yō megane

bifocals
遠近両用眼鏡
enkin ryōyō megane

hard/soft contact lenses
ハード／ソフトレン
ズ
hādo/sofuto renzu

conjunctivitis
結膜炎
ketsumakuen

stye
ものもらい
monomorai

cataracts
白内障
hakunaishō

blurred vision
かすみ目
kasumime

short-sighted
近視
kinshi

long-sighted
遠視
enshi

visually impaired
視覚障害者
shikaku shōgaisha

blind
目の不自由な
me no fujiyū-na

colour-blind
色盲の
shikimō no

to wear glasses
眼鏡を掛ける
megane o kakeru

to wear contacts
コンタクトを使う
kontakuto o tsukau

contact lenses
コンタクトレンズ
kontakuto renzu

contact lens case
コンタクトレンズケース
kontakuto renzu kēsu

eye chart
視力表
shiryoku hyō

eye drops
目薬
megusuri

eye test
視力検査
shiryoku kensa

frames
フレーム
furēmu

glasses
眼鏡
megane

glasses case
眼鏡ケース
megane kēsu

optician
眼鏡屋
megane-ya

The majority of hospitals and clinics are private, but public hospitals are more prestigious. Many accept Japanese national health insurance, but most accept payments only in cash.

### YOU MIGHT SAY...

Which ward is he/she in?
病棟はどこですか。
byōtō wa doko desu ka?

What are the visiting hours?
面会時間はいつですか。
menkai-jikan wa itsu desu ka?

### YOU MIGHT HEAR...

He/She is in ward...
…病棟です。
...byōtō desu.

Visiting hours are from ... to...
面会時間は…から…までです。
menkai-jikan wa ...kara ...made desu.

### VOCABULARY

public/private hospital
公立／私立病院
kōritsu/shiritsu byōin

A&E
救急医療科
kyūkyū iryōka

physiotherapist
理学療法士
rigaku ryōhōshi

radiographer
X線技師
ekkusu-sen gishi

surgeon
外科医
geka-i

operation
手術
shujutsu

scan
スキャン
sukyan

defibrillator
除細動器
josaidōki

intensive care
集中治療
shūchū chiryō

diagnosis
診断
shindan

to undergo surgery
手術を受ける
shujutsu o ukeru

to be admitted/
discharged
入院／退院する
nyūin/tai-in suru

### YOU SHOULD KNOW...

Call 119 for ambulance and fire and rescue – ambulances are dispatched from local fire stations. Air ambulances are called "Doctor Helicopters" and are staffed by doctors and nurses.

air ambulance
ドクターヘリ
dokutā heri

ambulance
救急車
kyūkyūsha

crutches
松葉づえ
matsubazue

drip
点滴
tenteki

hospital bed
病院ベッド
byōin beddo

monitor
モニター
monitā

operating theatre
手術室
shujutsu-shitsu

oxygen mask
酸素マスク
sanso masuku

ward
病棟
byōtō

wheelchair
車椅子
kuruma-isu

X-ray
レントゲン
rentogen

Zimmer frame®
歩行補助器
hokō hojoki

### YOU MIGHT SAY...

Can you call an ambulance?
救急車を呼んでください。
kyūkyūsha o yonde kudasai.

I've sprained my...
…をくじきました。
...o kujikimashita.

I've had an accident.
事故を起こしました。
jiko o okoshimashita.

I've cut myself.
切りました。
kirimashita.

I've hurt my...
…を痛めました。
...o itamemashita.

I've burnt myself.
やけどしました。
yakedo shimashita.

I've broken my...
…の骨を折りました。
...no hone o orimashita.

I've hit my head.
頭を打ちました。
atama o uchimashita.

### YOU MIGHT HEAR...

Do you feel dizzy?
気が遠くなりそうですか。
ki ga tōku nari-sō desu ka?

I've called an ambulance.
救急車を呼びました。
kyūkyūsha o yobimashita.

Do you feel sick?
吐き気がしますか。
hakike ga shimasu ka?

You need to be admitted.
入院してください。
nyūin shite kudasai.

### VOCABULARY

| | | |
|---|---|---|
| pulse 脈拍 myakuhaku | accident 事故 jiko | dislocation 脱臼 dakkyū |
| concussion 脳震とう nōshintō | fall 転落 tenraku | sprain 捻挫 nenza |

| scar | CPR | to take his/her pulse |
|------|-----|------------------------|
| 傷跡 | 心肺蘇生法 | 脈を測る |
| kizuato | shinpai sosēhō | myaku o hakaru |

| whiplash | neck brace | to injure oneself |
|----------|-----------|-------------------|
| むち打ち症 | けいつい装具 | けがをする |
| muchiuchishō | kētsui sōgu | kega o suru |

| swelling | plaster cast | to fall |
|----------|-------------|---------|
| むくみ | ギプス | 転落する |
| mukumi | gipusu | tenraku suru |

| tourniquet | splint | to break one's arm |
|-----------|--------|---------------------|
| 止血帯 | 添え木 | 腕を折る |
| shiketsutai | soegi | ude o oru |

| recovery position | to be unconscious | to twist one's ankle |
|--------------------|--------------------|------------------------|
| 回復体位 | 気を失っている | 足首をひねる |
| kaifuku tai-i | ki o ushinatte iru | ashikubi o hineru |

**INJURIES**

blister
まめ
mame

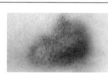

bruise
打ち身
uchimi

burn
火傷
yakedo

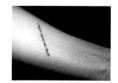

cut
切り傷
kirikizu

fracture
骨折
kossetsu

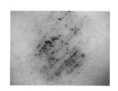

graze
擦り傷
surikizu

**splinter**
とげ
toge

**sting**
虫刺され
mushisasare

**sunburn**
日焼けの炎症
hiyake no enshō

**FIRST AID**

**adhesive tape**
絆創膏
bansōkō

**bandage**
包帯
hōtai

**first-aid kit**
救急箱
kyūkyūbako

**gauze**
ガーゼ
gāze

**ice pack**
氷のう
hyōnō

**ointment**
軟膏
nankō

**plaster**
救急絆創膏
kyūkyū bansōkō

**sling**
吊り包帯
tsuri hōtai

**tweezers**
ピンセット
pinsetto

Pharmacies are either individual shops or found in big department stores and supermarkets. They can provide advice and over-the-counter medicines for minor ailments as well as prescribed medicines.

## YOU MIGHT SAY...

I have a cold.
風邪をひきました。
kaze o hikimashita.

I have a temperature.
熱があります。
netsu ga arimasu.

I have flu.
インフルエンザにかかりました。
infuruenza ni kakarimashita.

I feel shivery/dizzy.
ぞくぞく／ふらふらします。
zokuzoku/furafura shimasu.

I have a rash.
発疹が出ました。
hasshin ga demashita.

I feel faint.
気が遠くなりそうです。
ki ga tōku nari-sō desu.

I have a sore stomach.
お腹が痛いです。
onaka ga itai desu.

I have asthma/diabetes.
喘息／糖尿病があります。
zensoku/tōnyōbyō ga arimasu.

## YOU MIGHT HEAR...

You should go to a pharmacy/clinic.
薬局／医者に行ったほうがいいですよ。
yakkyoku/isha ni itta hō ga ii desu yo.

You need to rest.
休んだほうがいいですよ。
yasunda hō ga ii desu yo.

## VOCABULARY

heart attack
心臓発作
shinzō hossa

infection
感染
kansen

virus
ウィールス
wiirusu

stroke
脳卒中
nōsotchū

ear infection
耳感染
mimi kansen

cold
風邪
kaze

flu
インフルエンザ
infuruenza

coeliac disease
セリアック病
seriakku-byō

insulin
インシュリン
inshurin

chicken pox
水ぼうそう
mizubōsō

diabetes
糖尿病
tōnyōbyō

period pain
生理痛
sēritsū

stomach bug
お腹の風邪
onaka no kaze

epilepsy
てんかん
tenkan

to have high/low blood pressure
血圧が高い／低い
ketsuatsu ga takai/hikui

food poisoning
食中毒
shokuchūdoku

asthma
喘息
zensoku

to cough
咳が出る
seki ga deru

vomiting
嘔吐
ōto

cancer
癌
gan

to sneeze
くしゃみをする
kushami o suru

diarrhoea
下痢
geri

migraine
偏頭痛
henzutsū

to vomit
吐く
haku

constipation
便秘
benpi

inhaler
吸入器
kyūnyūki

to faint
気が遠くなる
ki ga tōku naru

fever
熱
netsu

nausea
吐き気
hakike

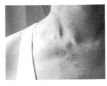

rash
発疹
hasshin

If you are travelling while pregnant, make sure you have appropriate travel insurance in place. If you become pregnant while living in Japan, register the pregnancy at your local municipal office, where you will receive a Mother and Child Health Handbook (母子手帳 boshi techō) and a health information package.

## YOU MIGHT SAY...

I'm 25 weeks pregnant.
妊娠 25週目です。
ninshin nijūgo-shū-me desu.

My partner/wife is pregnant.
パートナー／妻は妊娠してい
ます。
pātonā/tsuma wa ninshin shite imasu.

I'm/She's having contractions every ... minutes.
…分ごとに陣痛が来ます。
...fun/pun goto ni jintsū ga kimasu.

My/Her waters have broken.
破水しました。
hasui shimashita.

I need pain relief.
痛み止めがほしいです。
itami-dome ga hoshii desu.

## YOU MIGHT HEAR...

How far along are you?
何週目ですか。
nan-shū-me desu ka?

How long is it between contractions?
陣痛はどのぐらいの間隔です
か。
jintsū wa dono gurai no kankaku desu ka?

May I examine you?
診てみましょうか。
mite mimashō ka?

Push!
いきんで!
ikinde!

## VOCABULARY

foetus
胎児
taiji

uterus
子宮
shikyū

cervix
子宮頚部
shikyū kēbu

labour
陣痛
jintsū

delivery
分娩
bunben

epidural
硬膜外麻酔
kōmakugai-masui

| | | |
|---|---|---|
| Caesarean section<br>帝王切開<br>tēō sekkai | due date<br>予定日<br>yotēbi | to go into labour<br>陣痛が始まる<br>jintsū ga hajimaru |
| miscarriage<br>流産<br>ryūzan | morning sickness<br>つわり<br>tsuwari | to give birth<br>出産する<br>shussan suru |
| stillborn<br>死産<br>shizan | to get pregnant<br>妊娠する<br>ninshin suru | to miscarry<br>流産する<br>ryūzan suru |
| premature<br>未熟児<br>mijukuji | to be pregnant<br>妊娠している<br>ninshin shite iru | to breast-feed<br>授乳する<br>junyū suru |

**YOU SHOULD KNOW...**

Some hospitals may not tell you the baby's sex when you have a scan - you can also ask not to be told.

delivery room
分娩室
bunben-shitsu

incubator
保育器
hoikuki

midwife
助産婦
josanpu

newborn
新生児
shinsēji

pregnancy test
妊娠検査
ninshin kensa

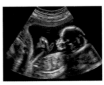

ultrasound
超音波
chō-onpa

Japan has a long history of using acupuncture and acupressure. Forest bathing – spending time in woodland as a form of therapy – has been popular in Japan since the 1980s.

## VOCABULARY

therapist
療法士
ryōhōshi

acupuncturist
鍼灸師
shinkyūshi

to relax
くつろぐ
kutsurogu

masseur/masseuse
マッサージ師
massājishi

reflexologist
リフロレクソロジスト
rifurekusorojisuto

to massage
マッサージする
massāji suru

chiropractor
カイロプラクター
kairopurakutā

doctor of Chinese medicine
漢方医
kanpōi

to meditate
めい想する
mēsō suru

forest bathing
森林浴
shinrin-yoku

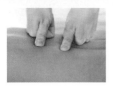
acupressure
指圧
shiatsu

acupuncture
鍼
hari

aromatherapy
アロマテラピー
aromaterapii

chiropractic
カイロプラクティック
kairopurakutikku

herbal medicine
ハーブ療法
hābu ryōhō

hypnotherapy
催眠療法
saimin ryōhō

massage
マッサージ
massāji

meditation
めい想
mēsō

moxibustion
灸
kyū

osteopathy
整骨療法
sēkotsu ryōhō

reflexology
リフレクソロジー
rifurekusorojii

traditional Chinese medicine
漢方薬
kanpōyaku

Bringing a pet to Japan is strictly regulated, and requires vaccinations against rabies and other diseases, microchipping, an import permit, and a quarantine period. You should check the requirements carefully beforehand.

### YOU MIGHT SAY...

I've got an appointment.
予約／約束があります。
yoyaku/yakusoku ga arimasu.

My dog has been hurt.
犬がけがをしました。
inu ga kega o shimashita.

My cat has been sick.
猫がずっと吐いています。
neko ga zutto haite imasu.

He/She keeps scratching.
いつもひっかいています。
itsumo hikkaite imasu.

### YOU MIGHT HEAR...

What's the problem?
どこが悪いですか。
doko ga warui desu ka?

Is your pet microchipped?
マイクロチップをしてありますか。
maikurochippu o shite arimasu ka?

Do you have an import quarantine certificate?
輸入検疫証明書はありますか。
yunyū ken'eki shōmēsho wa arimasu ka?

### VOCABULARY

veterinary clinic
動物病院
dōbutsu byōin

pet
ペット
petto

flea
ノミ
nomi

tick
ダニ
dani

quarantine
係留
kēryū

import permit
輸入許可証
yunyū kyokashō

rabies vaccination
狂犬病予防接種
kyōken-byō yobō-sesshu

microchip
マイクロチップ
maikurochippu

to vaccinate
予防接種をする
yobō-sesshu o suru

to spay/neuter
卵巣を除去／去勢する
ransō o jokyo/kyosē suru

to put to sleep
安楽死させる
anrakushi saseru

cage
ケージ
kēji

E-collar
エリザベスカラー
erizabesu karā

flea collar
ノミよけ首輪
nomiyoke kubiwa

lead
リード
riido

pet carrier
ペットキャリー
petto kyarii

veterinary nurse
獣医看護師
jūi kangoshi

vet
獣医
jūi

# PLANET EARTH | 地球

Japan's mountainous archipelago stretches approximately 1,500 miles, with a correspondingly wide range of scenery and climates. Over 30 national parks offer opportunities to explore mountain, forest, and marine environments.

crane
鶴
tsuru

wing
翼
tsubasa

beak
くちばし
kuchibashi

claw
つめ
tsume

tail
しっぽ
shippo

**YOU MIGHT SAY...**

What is the scenery like?
景色はどうですか。
keshiki wa dō desu ka?

**YOU MIGHT HEAR...**

The scenery is beautiful/rugged.
景色はきれい／岩だらけで
す。
keshiki wa kirē/iwa darake desu.

**VOCABULARY**

| | | |
|---|---|---|
| animal<br>動物<br>dōbutsu | fur<br>毛皮<br>kegawa | feather<br>羽<br>hane |
| bird<br>鳥<br>tori | paw/hoof<br>足<br>ashi | wings<br>翼<br>tsubasa |
| fish<br>魚<br>sakana | snout<br>鼻<br>hana | beak<br>くちばし<br>kuchibashi |
| species<br>種<br>shu | mane<br>たてがみ<br>tategami | scales<br>うろこ<br>uroko |
| national park<br>国立公園<br>kokuritsu kōen | tail<br>尾部<br>bibu | shell<br>貝殻<br>kaigara |
| nature reserve<br>自然保護区<br>shizen hogo-ku | claw<br>つめ<br>tsume | cold-blooded animal<br>変温動物<br>hen'on dōbutsu |
| zoo<br>動物園<br>dōbutsuen | horn<br>角<br>tsuno | warm-blooded animal<br>恒温動物<br>kōon dōbutsu |

Pet ownership is much lower than in the UK because homes are smaller and pets are often banned in apartments; cats and dogs are the most popular pets. The famous cat cafés have been joined by other animal cafés, although these have also prompted animal welfare concerns.

**YOU MIGHT SAY...**

Do you have any pets?
ペットを飼っていますか。
petto o katte imasu ka?

Is it OK to bring my pet?
ペットを連れてきてもいいですか。
petto o tsurete kite mo ii desu ka?

This is my guide dog/assistance dog.
これは私の盲導犬／身障者補助犬です。
kore wa watashi no mōdōken/shinshōsha hojoken desu.

What's the number for the vet?
獣医の電話番号は何ですか。
jūi no denwa-bangō wa nan desu ka?

My pet is missing.
ペットが行方不明になりました。
petto ga yukue fumē ni narimashita.

**YOU MIGHT HEAR...**

I have/don't have a pet.
ペットを飼っています／いません。
petto o katte imasu/imasen.

I'm allergic to pet hair.
ペットの毛にアレルギーがあります。
petto no ke ni arerugii ga arimasu.

Animals are/are not allowed.
動物は許されています／いません。
dōbutsu wa yurusarete imasu/imasen.

The phone number for the vet is...
獣医の電話番号は…です。
jūi no denwa-bangō wa ... desu.

"Beware of the dog".
「猛犬注意」
"mōken chūi".

**YOU SHOULD KNOW...**

Japan does not have a long history of farming animals, and it is therefore unusual to see cows and sheep grazing outside, apart from in Hokkaido and some other areas.

## VOCABULARY

fish food
魚のえさ
sakana no esa

cat litter
猫砂
neko suna

farmer
農家
nōka

farm
農場
nōjō

flock/herd
群れ
mure

animal feed
動物のえさ
dōbutsu no esa

kitten
子猫
koneko

puppy
子犬
koinu

to have a pet
ペットを飼う
petto o kau

to walk the dog
犬を散歩に連れて行く
inu o sanpo ni tsurete iku

to go to the vet
獣医に行く
jūi ni iku

to farm
養殖／飼育する
yōshoku/shiiku suru

## PETS

budgerigar
セキセイインコ
sekisē inko

canary
カナリア
kanaria

cat
猫
neko

dog
犬
inu

goldfish
金魚
kingyo

guinea pig
モルモット
morumotto

232

hamster
ハムスター
hamusutā

horse
馬
uma

rabbit
ウサギ
usagi

chicken
鶏
niwatori

cow
雌牛
meushi

duck
アヒル
ahiru

goat
ヤギ
yagi

pig
豚
buta

sheep
羊
hitsuji

aquarium
水槽
suisō

barn
納屋
naya

cage
ケージ
kēji

dog bed
犬用マットベッド
inu-yō matto beddo

goldfish bowl
金魚鉢
kingyo-bachi

hay
干し草
hoshikusa

hutch
ケージ
kēji

kennel
犬小屋
inu goya

litter tray
トイレトレー
toire torē

meadow
牧草地
bokusōchi

pet bowl
えさ入れ
esaire

pet food
ペットフード
petto fūdo

stable
馬小屋
umagoya

straw
わら
wara

trough
えさ入れ
esaire

alligator
ワニ
wani

crocodile
ワニ
wani

frog
カエル
kaeru

gecko
ヤモリ
yamori

iguana
イグアナ
iguana

lizard
トカゲ
tokage

newt
イモリ
imori

salamander
サンショウウオ
sanshōuo

snake
ヘビ
hebi

toad
ヒキガエル
hikigaeru

tortoise
カメ
kame

turtle
ウミガメ
umigame

bat
コウモリ
kōmori

boar
イノシシ
inoshishi

deer
シカ
shika

fox
キツネ
kitsune

hare
野ウサギ
nousagi

hedgehog
ハリネズミ
harinezumi

mouse
ネズミ
nezumi

raccoon dog
タヌキ
tanuki

squirrel
リス
risu

## OTHER COMMON MAMMALS

bear
クマ
kuma

bison
バイソン
baison

camel
ラクダ
rakuda

cheetah
チーター
chiitā

elephant
ゾウ
zō

giraffe
キリン
kirin

gorilla
ゴリラ
gorira

hippopotamus
カバ
kaba

leopard
ヒョウ
hyō

lion
ライオン
raion

monkey
サル
saru

reindeer
トナカイ
tonakai

rhinoceros
サイ
sai

tiger
トラ
tora

wolf
オオカミ
ōkami

black kite
トンビ
tonbi

buzzard
ノスリ
nosuri

cormorant
鵜
u

crane
ツル
tsuru

crow
カラス
karasu

cuckoo
カッコー
kakkō

dove
ハト
hato

eagle
ワシ
washi

egret
シラサギ
shirasagi

finch
フィンチ
finchi

gull
カモメ
kamome

heron
サギ
sagi

238

Japanese bush warbler
ウグイス
uguisu

kingfisher
カワセミ
kawasemi

lark
ヒバリ
hibari

murrelet
ウミスズメ
umi suzume

owl
フクロウ
fukurou

penguin
ペンギン
pengin

sparrow
スズメ
suzume

swallow
ツバメ
tsubame

swan
白鳥
hakuchō

tern
アジサシ
ajisashi

thrush
ツグミ
tsugumi

woodpecker
キツツキ
kitsutsuki

**VOCABULARY**

| | | |
|---|---|---|
| swarm<br>虫の群れ<br>mushi no mure | cobweb<br>クモの巣<br>kumo no su | to buzz<br>ブンブンいう<br>bunbun iu |
| colony<br>コロニー<br>koronii | insect bite<br>虫刺され<br>mushi-sasare | to sting<br>刺す<br>sasu |

ant
アリ
ari

bee
ミツバチ
mitsubachi

beetle
カブトムシ
kabutomushi

butterfly
チョウ
chō

caterpillar
イモムシ
imomushi

centipede
ムカデ
mukade

cicada
セミ
semi

cockroach
アブラムシ
aburamushi

cricket
コオロギ
kōrogi

dragonfly
トンボ
tonbo

earthworm
ミミズ
mimizu

firefly
蛍
hotaru

fly
ハエ
hae

hornet
オオスズメバチ
ōsuzumebachi

ladybird
テントウ虫
tentōmushi

mosquito
蚊
ka

moth
蛾
ga

slug
ナメクジ
namekuji

snail
カタツムリ
katatsumuri

spider
クモ
kumo

wasp
スズメバチ
suzumebachi

241

coral
珊瑚
sango

crab
カニ
kani

dolphin
イルカ
iruka

eel
ウナギ
unagi

jellyfish
クラゲ
kurage

lobster
ロブスター
robusutā

seahorse
タツノオトシゴ
tatsu no otoshigo

seal
アザラシ
azarashi

sea urchin
ウニ
uni

shark
サメ
same

starfish
ヒトデ
hitode

whale
クジラ
kujira

## VOCABULARY

| | | |
|---|---|---|
| stalk<br>茎<br>kuki | petal<br>花びら<br>hanabira | seed<br>種<br>tane |
| leaf<br>葉<br>ha | bud<br>芽<br>me | bulb<br>球根<br>kyūkon |

## YOU SHOULD KNOW...

The chrysanthemum symbolizes the imperial family and is associated with autumn. Some other flowers, most famously the spring cherry blossom, are also strongly associated with the seasons.

buttercup
キンポウゲ
kinpōge

chrysanthemum
菊
kiku

daffodil
ラッパズイセン
rappazuisen

daisy
ヒナギク
hinagiku

dandelion
タンポポ
tanpopo

iris
アヤメ
ayame

lavender
ラベンダー
rabendā

lily
ユリ
yuri

lily-of-the-valley
スズラン
suzuran

morning glory
朝顔
asagao

orchid
ラン
ran

pansy
パンジー
panjii

peony
ボタン
botan

poppy
ケシ
keshi

rose
バラ
bara

sunflower
ヒマワリ
himawari

tulip
チューリップ
chūrippu

violet
スミレ
sumire

## VOCABULARY

branch
枝
eda

bark
木の皮
ki no kawa

root
根
ne

trunk
幹
miki

berry
ベリー
berii

orchard
果樹園
kajuen

bamboo
竹
take

broom
エニシダ
enishida

camellia
椿
tsubaki

cedar
杉
sugi

cherry tree
桜
sakura

chestnut tree
栗
kuri

fir
モミ
momi

fungus
菌類
kinrui

gingko
イチョウ
ichō

grapevine
ブドウの木
budō no ki

grass
草
kusa

honeysuckle
スイカズラ
suikazura

ivy
ツタ
tsuta

Japanese pampas grass
ススキ
susuki

katsura
桂
katsura

lichen
地衣類
chiirui

maple
カエデ
kaede

moss
苔
koke

pine
マツ
matsu

willow
ヤナギ
yanagi

wisteria
藤
fuji

## VOCABULARY

| | | |
|---|---|---|
| scenery<br>景色<br>keshiki | water<br>水<br>mizu | sunset<br>日の入り<br>hi no iri |
| landscape<br>景色<br>keshiki | estuary<br>入り江<br>irie | rural<br>田舎の<br>inaka no |
| wood<br>林<br>hayashi | pond<br>池<br>ike | urban<br>都会の<br>tokai no |
| cave<br>洞穴<br>dōketsu | air<br>空気<br>kūki | polar<br>北極、南極の<br>hokkyoku, nankyoku no |
| soil<br>土<br>tsuchi | atmosphere<br>大気<br>taiki | alpine<br>高山の<br>kōzan no |
| mud<br>泥<br>doro | sunrise<br>日の出<br>hinode | tropical<br>熱帯の<br>nettai no |

## LAND

desert
砂漠
sabaku

farmland
農地
nōchi

forest
森林
shinrin

glacier
氷河
hyōga

grassland
草原
sōgen

hill
丘
oka

lake
湖
mizu umi

marsh
湿地
shitchi

mountain
山
yama

river
川
kawa

rocks
岩
iwa

scrub
雑木林
zōki-bayashi

stream
小川
ogawa

valley
谷
tani

waterfall
滝
taki

# SEA

cliff
崖
gake

coast
海岸
kaigan

coral reef
サンゴ礁
sangoshō

island
島
shima

peninsula
半島
hantō

rockpool
潮だまり
shiodamari

# SKY

aurora
オーロラ
ōrora

clouds
雲
kumo

moon
月
tsuki

rainbow
虹
niji

stars
星
hoshi

sun
太陽
taiyō

Japan's location on the Pacific Ring of Fire makes it subject to earthquakes and tsunamis, and in typhoon season (mainly August and September), heavy rainfall can cause floods and landslides. Public warnings (警報 keihō) are issued via loudspeakers, radio, TV, and the internet, and an app gives alerts in English.

## VOCABULARY

aftershock
余震
yoshin

flash flood
鉄砲水
teppōmizu

volcano
火山
kazan

lava
溶岩
yōgan

avalanche
雪崩
nadare

forest fire
山火事
yama-kaji

rescue team
救助隊
kyūjo-tai

to evacuate
避難する
hinan suru

to rescue
救助する
kyūjo suru

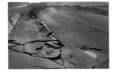

earthquake
地震
jishin

flood
洪水
kōzui

landslide
崖くずれ／地すべり
gakekuzure/jisuberi

tsunami
津波
tsunami

typhoon
台風
taifū

volcanic eruption
噴火
funka

# CELEBRATIONS AND FESTIVALS | お祝いと祭り

Although Japanese people are known for being hard-working, they also like to celebrate important life events and to enjoy themselves. Japan has 16 national holidays, marking events such as the Emperor's birthday and spring and autumn equinoxes. Other national holidays celebrate children, older people, culture, and sports. There is a wealth of Japanese customs and traditions associated with the various holidays and festivals.

Japanese national dress
日本の民族衣装
nihon no minzoku ishō

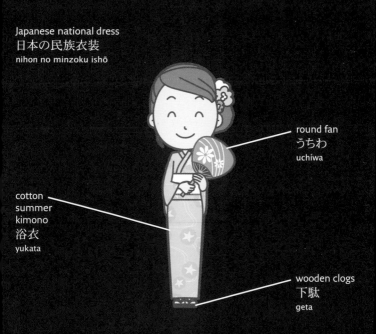

round fan
うちわ
uchiwa

cotton
summer
kimono
浴衣
yukata

wooden clogs
下駄
geta

## YOU MIGHT SAY/HEAR...

| | |
|---|---|
| Congratulations!<br>おめでとう（ございます）！<br>omedetō (gozaimasu)! | Happy birthday!<br>誕生日おめでとう！<br>tanjōbi omedetō! |
| Well done!<br>よくやったね！<br>yoku yatta ne! | Good luck!<br>がんばってください！<br>ganbatte kudasai! |
| Cheers!<br>乾杯！<br>kanpai! | Thank you.<br>ありがとう（ございます）。<br>arigatō (gozaimasu). |

## VOCABULARY

| | | |
|---|---|---|
| occasion<br>特別な出来事<br>tokubetsu-na dekigoto | wedding anniversary<br>結婚記念日<br>kekkon kinenbi | greetings card<br>カード<br>kādo |
| birthday<br>誕生日<br>tanjōbi | public holiday<br>祝祭日<br>shukusaijitsu | to celebrate<br>祝う<br>iwau |
| 60th birthday<br>還暦<br>kanreki | celebration<br>お祝い<br>o-iwai | to throw a party<br>パーティーをする<br>pātii o suru |
| wedding<br>結婚式<br>kekkon-shiki | good/bad news<br>いい／悪い 知らせ<br>ii/warui shirase | to toast<br>乾杯する<br>kanpai suru |

## YOU SHOULD KNOW...

Although wedding ceremonies have traditionally been Shinto, western Christian-style weddings are becoming increasingly popular but generally do not imply Christian beliefs.

bouquet
花束
hanataba

chocolates
チョコレート
chokorēto

cake
ケーキ
kēki

fireworks
花火
hanabi

gift
贈り物
okurimono

karaoke
カラオケ
karaoke

party
パーティー
pātii

Shinto and Buddhism co-exist, alongside small populations of Christians and followers of new religions. Shinto rituals are associated with birth and life, but funerals are usually Buddhist.

## VOCABULARY

birth
誕生
tanjō

childhood
子供時代
kodomo jidai

passing your driving test
運転免許を取る
unten menkyo o toru

school entrance ceremony
入学式
nyūgaku-shiki

graduation
卒業
sotsugyō

finding a job
就職
shūshoku

falling in love
恋をする
koi o suru

engagement
婚約
kon'yaku

marriage
結婚
kekkon

divorce
離婚
rikon

becoming a parent
親になる
oya ni naru

getting a new job
転職
tenshoku

first shrine visit
お宮参り／初宮参り
o-miyamairi/hatsu miyamairi

moving house
引っ越し
hikkoshi

relocation
転勤
tenkin

retirement
退職
taishoku

funeral
葬式
sōshiki

gift envelope
祝儀袋
shūgibukuro

## YOU SHOULD KNOW...

It is customary to give money rather than gifts on both happy and sad occasions. Celebration money is called お祝儀 (o-shūgi) and condolences money is 不祝儀 (bushūgi). It is put into gift envelopes which are decorated appropriately for the occasion and amount of money.

There are thousands of festivals throughout the year, ranging from small-scale local ones to major events that attract thousands of people. They are often linked to agriculture and the seasons, for example, harvest festivals and Shinto practices. Processions are common, with beautifully decorated floats, musicians, and a portable shrine (神輿 mikoshi) carrying the local Shinto deity (神 kami) around the area.

## YOU MIGHT SAY/HEAR...

Is it a holiday today?
今日は祝日ですか。
kyō wa shukujitsu desu ka?

And to you, too!
…さんも。
...san mo!

Merry Christmas!
メリークリスマス!
merii kurisumasu!

What are your plans for the holiday?
休みに何をするつもりですか。
yasumi ni nani o suru tsumori desu ka?

## VOCABULARY

Coming of Age Day
成人の日
sējin no hi

April Fool's Day
エイプリルフール
eipurīru fūru

Christmas Day
クリスマス
kurisumasu

Mother's Day
母の日
haha no hi

May Day
メーデー
mēdē

Valentine's Day
バレンタインデー
barentain dē

Father's Day
父の日
chichi no hi

Christmas Eve
クリスマスイブ
kurisumasu ibu

Halloween
ハロウィーン
harowiin

## YOU SHOULD KNOW...

The beauty of cherry blossom has been celebrated in Japan for centuries and draws visitors from all over the world. March and April are the main months for cherry blossom viewing, with parties held under the trees, and weather forecasts include reports on the progress of the 'cherry blossom front' 桜前線 (sakura zensen) from south to north.

Children are the focus of several annual festivals. On 3 March, Girls' Day
(ひな祭り hina matsuri) is celebrated with special food and a display of dolls.
Children's Day (formerly Boys' Day) is a public holiday on 5 May, marked
by carp streamers flying from roofs to symbolize courage and strength.
In November, children aged 3, 5, and 7 are dressed formally and taken
to their local Shinto shrine to offer thanks and pray for their future health
and happiness.

autumn leaves viewing
紅葉狩り
momijigari

Bon Festival of the Dead
お盆
o-bon

carp streamer
鯉のぼり
koinobori

cherry blossom viewing
（お）花見
(o-)hanami

Coming of Age Day
成人の日
sējin no hi

floating lantern
灯篭流し
tōrō-nagashi

Moon Viewing Festival
（お）月見
(o-)tsukimi

7-5-3 Festival
七五三
shichi go san

Star Festival
七夕
tanabata

New Year is the most important holiday, when families gather and celebrate together. Shops, businesses, and tourist attractions used to close for several days around New Year, but many shops now stay open except for (but sometimes including) 1 January.

## VOCABULARY

New Year's Eve
大晦日
ōmisoka

New Year's Day
元旦
gantan

Happy New Year!
明けましておめでとうございます。
akemashite omedetō gozaimasu.

## YOU SHOULD KNOW...

Temple bells are struck 108 times at midnight on 31 December, symbolizing the number of worldly temptations that lead to suffering, according to Buddhist beliefs. People visit their local temple or shrine in the first few days of January to wish for good luck, health, and success in the coming year.

New Year shrine visit
初詣
hatsumōde

Chinese New Year
旧正月
kyūshōgatsu

end-of-year party
忘年会
bōnenkai

New Year card
年賀状
nengajō

New Year food
お節料理
o-sechi ryōri

New Year money
お年玉
o-toshidama

New Year's Eve temple bell
除夜の鐘
joya no kane

spiced sake
お屠蘇
o-toso

pine and bamboo decoration
門松
kadomatsu

sticky rice cake
(お)もち
(o-)mochi

258

# INDEX | 索引

## ENGLISH

abalone 98
abdomen 206
ABOUT YOU 9
accessible parking
    space 27
accessories 111
ACCOMMODATION
    159
accordion 168
account passbook
    146
acoustic guitar 168
acupressure 226
acupuncture 226
adhesive tape 220
adzuki bean bun 92
aeroplane 46
aikido 196
air ambulance 217
airbag 32
airport 46
alarm clock 68
alligator 235
ALTERNATIVE
    THERAPIES 225
aluminium foil 62
ambulance 217
American football
    200
AMPHIBIANS AND
    REPTILES 235
anchor 49
anime film 157
ankle 205
ant 240
antifreeze 32
antiperspirant 106
antiques shop 119
antiseptic cream 105
apartment block 53
apple 86
apprentice geisha
    157
aquarium 233
arm 206
armbands 188
armchair 61
aromatherapy 226
art gallery 155
ARTS AND CRAFTS 174
ashtray 130
asparagus 89
assistant referee 185

athlete 198
ATHLETICS 198
ATM 146
aubergine 89
aurora 249
automatic door 33
autumn leaves
    viewing 256
avocado 86
azuki bean jelly 128
baby food 108
BABY GOODS 108
baby's bottle 108
baby seat 109
baby shoes 108
baby sling 109
back 207
bacon 95
badminton 190
badminton racket
    190
baggage reclaim 46
bags 111
baguette 92
BAKERY 92
baking tray 63
balcony 51
ball boy 191
ball girl 191
ball of wool 174
bamboo 245
bamboo shoots 89
bamboo sword 196
banana 75, 86
bandage 105, 201,
    220
BANK 145
banknotes 78, 146
bar 157
barber's 119
barley tea 83
barn 233
BASEBALL 182
baseball 182
baseball bat 182
baseball cap 182
baseball game 182
baseball mitt 182
baseball player 182
BASICS 8, 20, 52, 76,
    122, 152, 178,
    202, 230, 252
basket 75, 80, 183
BASKETBALL 183

basketball 183
basketball court 183
basketball game 183
basketball player 183
basketball shoes 183
bass guitar 168
bat 236
bath 70
BATHROOM 70
bathroom 70
bath stool 163
BEACH 165
beach ball 166
beak 229
bean curd 80
bear 236
beauty salon 120
bed 69
bedding 68
BEDROOM 68
bedroom 69
bedside table 69
bee 240
beefburger 95
beef cooked in stock
    with dipping
    sauce 126
beef hotpot cooked
    in sweetened
    stock 126
beer 83
beer mug 130
beetle 240
bell 39
belt 116
bento box 133
bib 108
BICYCLE 38
bicycle 38
big toe 205
bike lock 39
bikini 166
bill 130
bin bag 62
BIRDS 238
bison 236
black 7
blackboard 139
black coffee 123
black kite 238
black tea 83, 123
blade 19
blanket 68
blind 60

blister 219
block of flats 51
blood pressure
    monitor 211
blouse 114
blue 7
blueberry 86
blue cheese 100
Bluetooth® headset
    136
Bluetooth® speaker
    168
Blu-ray® player 60
blusher 107
boar 236
boarding card 47
BODY 204
body 206, 207
bodysuit 108
boiler 55
Bon Festival of the
    Dead 256
bonito 97
bonnet 26
bonsai 176
bonsai scissors 72
bookcase 61
bookshop 119
boot 26
boots 37, 117
bouquet 253
box 148
boxed lunch 42
boxer shorts 114
boxing 196
bra 114
bracelet 116
braces 213
brake 39
bread 75, 123
breaded pork cutlet
    126
bread rolls 92
BREAKFAST 123
breastbone 209
bridge 27
brioche 93
broccoli 89
broom 245
brown rice 80
brown rice green tea
    84
bruise 219
brush 73

bucket 73
buckwheat noodles
    80, 126
Buddhist temple
    149, 155
budgerigar 232
bullet train 42
bumper 26
bunk beds 68
bunraku puppet
    theatre 158
buoy 49
bureau de change
    146
burger 133
burn 219
BUS AND TRAM 34
bus station 36
bus stop 36
bus ticket 36
BUTCHER'S 94
butter 100
buttercup 243
butterfly 240
buttock 207
buttons 174
buzzard 238
buzzer 36
cabbage 89
cabin 47
café 149
cafeteria 141
cafetière 63
cage 228, 233
cake 253
calculator 139
calf 207
calligraphy 176
calligraphy brush,
    inkstick, inkstone
    176
camel 236
camellia 245
camera lens 171
CAMPING 164
campus 141
canal 49
canary 232
canoe 50
canoeing 188
capsule 105
capsule hotel 161
CAR 22

car 26
cardigan 114
card reader 78
cards 172
car park 27
carp streamer 256
carriage 42
carrot 89
CAR TROUBLE 30
car wash 28
castle 155
cat 232
caterpillar 240
cathedral 155
cauliflower 89
cedar 245
celery 89
cello 168
centipede 240
centre circle 177
cereal 123
chain 39
chair 131
changing bag 108
changing room 181
charger 136
check-in desk 47
cheddar 100
cheek 205
cheetah 237
cherry 86
cherry blossom
  viewing 256
cherry tree 245
chess 172
chest 206
chestnut 86
chestnut tree 245
chest of drawers 69
chicken 233
chicken and egg on
  rice 126
chicken yakitori 133
Children's Day 256
chilli 89
chin 205
Chinese cabbage 89
Chinese New Year
  257
Chinese noodles 80,
  126
Chinese-style
  dumplings 126
chips 127
chiropractic 226
chocolate 83
chocolates 253
choir 170
chopping board
  63

chopstick rest 66,
  131
chopsticks 66, 131
chrysanthemum 243
church 149
cicada 240
cigarette 102
cinema 158
city hall 149
city map 155
clam 98
clarinet 168
claw 229
cliff 249
clingfilm 62
cloth 73
clothes horse 73
clothes pegs 73
CLOTHING 112
clouds 249
coach 36, 42
coast 249
coastguard boat 50
coat 114
coat hanger 68
cockpit 19, 47
cockroach 240
cod 97
coffee jelly 128
coffee shop 144
coffee table 61
coins 78
colander 63
collarbone 209
colouring pencils 139
comb 107
comic storytelling
  158
COMMUNICATION AND
  IT 135
community police
  post 149
compact camera 171
compass 194
computer 136
concert 158
condom 105
conductor 170
conference centre
  149
contact lens case 215
contact lenses 215
cooked vegetables
  127
cooking 153
coral 242
coral reef 249
corkscrew 63
cormorant 238

corridor 161
cosmetics 111
cosplay 158
cot 109
cottage cheese 100
cotton bud 109
cotton hand towel
  101
cotton kimono 163
cotton summer
  kimono 113, 251
cough mixture 105
counters 172
courgette 89
courthouse 150
court shoes 117
cow 233
crab 98, 242
crampons 194
crane 229, 238
crash helmet 37
cream 100
credit card 78, 146
crème caramel 128
cricket 200, 240
crisps 83
crochet hook 174
crocodile 235
croissant 93, 123
crossbar 39
cross trainer 181
crow 238
crutches 217
cuckoo 238
cucumber 89
cup 121
cup and saucer 66
cupboard 65
curling 200
curry bun 93
curry with rice 126
curtains 60, 69
cushion 61
cut 219
daffodil 243
daisy 243
dandelion 243
Danish pastry 93
Daruma doll 107
dashboard 24
DAYS, MONTHS, AND
  SEASONS 16
debit card 78, 146
deer 236
delivery room 224
dental floss 213
dental nurse 213
dentist 213
dentist's chair 213
dentist's drill 213

DENTIST'S SURGERY
  212
dentures 213
DEPARTMENT STORE
  110
departure board 47
desert 247
desk 143
desk lamp 143
detached house 53
dice 173
DINING AT HOME 66
discount shop 119
discus 198
dishwasher 73
diver 188
diving board 188
DIY 153
DIY STORE 118
doctor 203
dog 232
dog bed 234
doll 101
dolphin 242
DOMESTIC ANIMALS
  AND BIRDS 231
door 26
doorbell 58
double bass 168
double room 161
doughnut 93
dove 238
dragonfly 241
draining board 65
drainpipe 58
drawer 65, 69
dress 114
dressing table 68
dried bonito flakes
  80
drip 217
driver 33
DRIVING 26
driving range 195
drops 105
drum kit 169
DSLR camera 171
duck 95, 233
dumbbell 181
dustbin 74
dustpan 74
duty-free shop 47
duvet 69
DVD player 60
eagle 238
ear 205
earphones 168
earrings 116
earthquake 250
earthworm 241

EATING OUT 129
éclair 93
E-collar 228
EDUCATION 138
eel 97, 242
egg 100
egret 238
elbow 207
electrical store 119
electric fan 60
electric guitar 169
electronics 111
electronics store 119
elephant 237
embroidery 175
emergency phone 32
end-of-year party
  257
energy drink 102
ENTERTAINMENT 156
entrance curtain 163
ENTRANCE HALL 57
envelope 103, 148
eraser 140
examination table
  211
exchange rate 146
exercise bike 181
exercise book 140
extension cable 55
eye 205
eye chart 215
eye drops 215
eyeliner 107
eyeshadow 107
eye test 215
fabric 174
fabric scissors 174
face 205, 206
FAMILY AND FRIENDS
  10
farmhouse 53
farmland 247
fashion 111
FAST FOOD 133
femur 209
fence 71
fermented soy beans
  80, 124
ferry 50
FERRY AND BOAT
  TRAVEL 48
festival 158
FESTIVALS 255
fever 222
fibula 209
fig 87
filing cabinet 143
finch 238
finger 205

fingernail 205
fir 245
firefly 241
fire station 150
fireworks 253
first-aid kit 201, 220
fish slice 63
FISHMONGER'S 96
FITNESS 180
fizzy drink 84
flavoured shaved ice 128
flea collar 228
flip-flops 117
floating lantern 256
flood 250
floor 61
floor cushion 59, 131
florist's 120
flounder 97
flower arranging 176
flowerpot 71
FLOWERS 243
flowers 71, 176
flute 169
fly 241
flysheet 151
folder 143
folding fan 101
food and drink 111
food processor 63
foot 205, 206
FOOTBALL 184
football 185
football boots 185
football match 185
football pitch 177, 185
football player 185
footbath 163
footwear 111
forehead 205
forest 247
forest bathing 225
formula milk 109
foundation 107
fox 236
fracture 219
frame 39
frames 215
FRESH AND DAIRY PRODUCTS 100
fridge-freezer 65
fried tofu and rice balls 134
fries 134
frog 235
front light 39
FRUIT AND VEGETABLES 86

fruit juice 84
fruit parfait 128
frying pan 63
fuel gauge 24
fuel pump 28
funfair 158
fungus 245
furniture 111
furniture store 120
fusebox 55
futon 59
game controller 173
GAMES 172
games console 173
gaming 153
gangway 49
garage 32
GARDEN 71
garden 71
garden fork 72
garden hose 72
gardening 153
gardening gloves 72
gardens 155
garlic 90
gate 56
gateball 200
gauze 220
gears 39
gearstick 24
gecko 235
GENERAL HEALTH AND WELLBEING 12
gift 253
gift envelope 103
gifts 111
GIFTS AND SOUVENIRS 101
ginger 90
gingko 245
giraffe 237
glacier 248
glass 131
glasses 215
glasses case 215
glove compartment 25
gloves 116
go 173
goal 177, 185
goalkeeper 185
goalkeeper's gloves 185
goalposts 186
goat 233
goggles 188
goldfish 232
goldfish bowl 234
GOLF 195
golf bag 195

golf ball 195
golf buggy 195
golf club 195
gorilla 237
grape 87
grapefruit 87
grapevine 245
grass 245
grassland 248
grater 63
gratin 127
graze 219
green 7
green beans 90
green tea 84, 124
greetings card 103
grilled eel on rice 126
grilled fish 124
ground coffee 84
groundsheet 151
guidebook 155
guinea pig 232
gull 238
gums 213
gutter 56
guy rope 151
gym ball 181
gymnastics 200
hair 205
hairbrush 107
hairdresser's 120
hairdryer 69
ham 95
hammer 118
hamster 233
hand 205, 206
handbag 116
handbrake 25
hand drum 170
handle 121
handlebars 39
hand mixer 63
hanging scroll 59
happi festival coat 113
harbour 49
hard-boiled egg 124
hare 236
harp 169
hat 108
hay 234
head 206
headlight 26
headphones 168
headrest 25
health food shop 120
heated table 59
heater 56
hedgehog 236
heel 205

helicopter 19
helmet 39
herbal medicine 226
herbs 82
heron 238
herring 97
highchair 109
high heels 117
high jump 198
highlighter 140
hijiki seaweed 80
hill 248
hip 207
hippopotamus 237
hi-viz vest 32
hob 65
holdall 47
hole punch 140
homeware 111
honey 82
honeysuckle 246
hornet 241
horse 233
horse mackerel 97
horse racing 200
HOSPITAL 216
hospital 150, 203
hospital bed 217
hostel 161
hot dog 134
hotel 53, 150
hot spring 163
HOT SPRINGS 162
HOUSE 54
HOUSEWORK 73
humerus 209
hurdles 199
hutch 234
hypnotherapy 226
ice axe 194
ice cream 83, 128
iced coffee 84
ice hockey 200
ice pack 220
ice skates 193
ice skating 193
ignition 25
iguana 235
ILLNESS 221
incubator 224
indicator 26
inflatable dinghy 50
information board 42
injury 218
ink cartridge 143
ink painting 176
in/out tray 143
insect repellent 106
INSIDE THE BODY 208

instant coffee 84
intercom 58
IN TOWN 149
iris 243
iron 74
ironing board 74
island 249
ivy 246
jack 32
jacket 114
jam 82, 124
Japanese abacus 140
Japanese archery 197
Japanese bush warbler 239
Japanese cake 176
Japanese drum 170
Japanese dumpling 83
Japanese fishcake 80
Japanese flute 170
Japanese hotpot 126
Japanese inn 161
Japanese lute 170
Japanese mushrooms 90
Japanese national dress 251
Japanese pampas grass 246
Japanese paper 176
Japanese pear 87
JAPANESE ROOM 59
Japanese stew 134
Japanese stock 80
Japanese stuffed pancake 83
Japanese-style rice 126
Japanese teacup 131
Japanese teapot 66
Japanese towel 70
Japanese veranda 59
javelin 199
jaw 205
jeans 114
jellyfish 99, 242
jet ski 188
jetty 49
jeweller's 120
jigsaw puzzle 173
jogging 153
jogging bottoms 115
judo 197
jumper 115
jump leads 32
junction 28
kabuki 158
karaoke 158, 253
karate 197

katsura 246
kayak 50
kayaking 188
keirin 200
kelp 81
kendo 197
kennel 234
ketchup 82
kettle 63
kettle bell 181
keyboard 169
key card 161
kimono 113
kingfisher 239
KITCHEN 62
kitchen 65
kitchen knife 63
kitchen roll 62
kiwi fruit 87
knee 206
kneecap 209
knee protectors 37
knife and fork 66, 131
knitting needles 174
knuckle 205
koto 170
lace-up shoes 117
lacquerware 101
ladle 64
ladybird 241
lake 248
LAND, SEA, AND SKY
247
landslide 250
lane 28
laptop 144
lark 239
laundrette 150
laundry basket 69
laundry pole 74
lavender 244
lawn 71
lawnmower 72
lead 228
leather gloves 37
leather jacket 37
lecture hall 141
lecturer 141
leek 90
leg 206
leggings 115
legless chair 59
leisure centre 179
lemon 87
lemon sole 97
leopard 237
letter 148
lettuce 90
level crossing 28
library 141, 150

lichen 246
lifebuoy 50
LIFE EVENTS 254
lifeguard 166
lifejacket 50, 189
lift 58
light bulb 56
lily 244
lily-of-the-valley
244
line judge 191
liner 50
lingerie 111
lion 237
lipstick 107
listening to music
153
litter tray 234
lizard 235
lobster 99, 242
locker 181
locomotive 42
loincloth 197
long jump 199
loquat 87
lotus root 90
LOUNGE 60
lounge 61
lower back 207
low table 59, 131
lozenge 106
luggage locker 42
luggage rack 43
luggage trolley 47
mackerel 97
magazine 102
MAIN MEALS 125
maki rolls 134
MAMMALS 236
mango 87
map 21
maple 246
MARINE CREATURES
242
MARKET 85
marsh 248
MARTIAL ARTS AND
SUMO 196
mascara 107
massage 226
matcha green tea
176
mattress 69
mayonnaise 82
meadow 234
measuring jug 64
mechanic 32
mechanical pencil
140
medal 179

MEDICAL
APPOINTMENT 210
meditation 226
melon 87
menu 131
meter 56
metro 43
microwave 65
midwife 224
milk 100
mince 95
mineral water 84
minibar 161
minibus 36
MINIBEASTS 240
mirror 69, 70
miso soup 124, 126
miso soup bowl 66,
131
mittens 108
mixing bowl 64
model-making 175
moist towel 131
monitor 217
monkey 237
monkfish 97
monorail 43
mooli 90
moon 249
Moon Viewing
Festival 256
mooring 50
mop 74
morning glory 244
mosque 150
mosquito 241
moss 246
moth 241
MOTORBIKE 37
motorbike 37
motor racing 200
motorway 28
mountain 248
mouse 236
mouse mat 137
mouth 205
mouth organ 169
moxibustion 226
mozzarella 100
murrelet 239
museum 150
MUSIC 167
musical 158
musician 170
music shop 120
mussel 99
mustard 82
nails 118
nail varnish 107

napkin 67
nappy 109
nappy cream 109
NATURAL DISASTERS
250
nausea 222
navel orange 87
neck 206
necklace 116
nectarine 87
needle and thread
174
NEW YEAR 257
New Year card 257
New Year food 257
New Year money 257
New Year's Eve
temple bell 257
New Year shrine visit
257
newborn 224
newspaper 102
newt 235
Noh 158
nori seaweed sheets
81
nose 19, 205
notebook 103
notepad 144
number plate 26
nurse 203
nuts 83
oars 189
octopus 99
octopus dumplings
134
OFFICE 142
office block 150
off-licence 120
oil paint 175
oil-paper umbrella
101
ointment 106
olive oil 75, 82
omelette 127
onigiri 124
onion 90
operating theatre
217
optician 215
OPTICIAN'S 214
optician's 120
orange 87
orange juice 124
orchestra 170
orchid 244
origami 176
origami paper 101
osteopathy 226
OTHER SHOPS 119

OTHER SPORTS 200
outdoor bath 163
oven 65
owl 239
oxygen mask 217
oyster 99
Pacific saury 97
package 148
padded envelope 148
paddle 189
paddleboarding 189
paint 118
paintbrush 118
pak choi 90
palm 205
pancakes 93
pansy 244
pants 115
papaya 88
paper 140
paper clip 144
paper wall panel 59
paramedic 203
park 150
parking space 28
party 253
passport 47
pasta 82, 127
path 71
pavement 28
peach 88
peas 90
pedal 39
pedal bin 62
pedestrian crossing
28
peeler 64
peephole 58
pelvis 209
pen 102, 140
penalty box 177
pencil 103, 140
pencil case 140
penguin 239
peninsula 249
peony 244
pepper 82
persimmon 88
pet bowl 234
pet carrier 228
pet food 234
petrol station 28
pet shop 120
pharmacist 203
PHARMACY 104
pharmacy 203
phone case 137
photocopier 144
PHOTOGRAPHY 171
piano 169

pickled plums 81, 124
pickled vegetables 81
picture postcard 103, 148
pig 233
pill 106
pillow 69
pilot 47
pine 246
pine and bamboo decoration 257
pineapple 88
pins 175
pizza 127
plaster 106, 201, 220
plastic bag 78
plate 67, 131
platform 43
playground 150
plum 88
podium 179
pole vault 199
police officer 28
police station 150
pomegranate 88
popcorn 83
poppy 244
postal worker 148
postbox 148
POST OFFICE 147
potato 91
potatoes 128
pottery 175
potty 109
power pack 137
pram 109
prawn 99
PREGNANCY 223
pregnancy test 224
printer 144
pruners 72
public housing complex 53
pump 39
purse 116
pushchair 109
pyjamas 115

rabbit 233
raccoon dog 236
RACKET SPORTS 190
radio 60
radius 209
RAIL TRAVEL 40
railway station 43
rainbow 249
rainbow trout 97
rake 72
rash 222
raw vegetables 128

razor 106
reading 153
rearview mirror 25
receipt 78
reception 161
red 7
red card 185
redcurrant 88
red pepper 91
(red/white/mixed) soy bean paste 81
referee 179
reflector 39
reflexology 226
reindeer 237
remote control 60
rhinoceros 237
ribs 95, 209
rice 81
rice bowl 67, 132
rice cooker 64
rice crackers 83
rice porridge 124
rice vinegar 81
ring binder 140
river 248
road 28
roadworks 29
roasted green tea 84
rockpool 249
rocks 248
rolled omelette 124
rolling pin 64
roof 26, 51, 56
rope 194
rose 244
rotor 19
roundabout 29
round fan 101, 251
rowing boat 50
rowing machine 181
rubber gloves 74
rug 69
RUGBY 186
rugby 186
rugby ball 186
rugby field 186
rugby player 186
ruler 140
running track 199
runway 47
saddle 39
safe 161
safety pin 175
sailing boat 50, 189
sake 84
sake cup 67
sake cup and flask 132
sake flask 67

salad 128
salad bowl 67
salamander 235
salmon 97
salt 82
salt and pepper 132
sandals 117
sandwich 134
sanitary towel 106
sardine 98
sash 114
sashimi 127
sat nav 25
satsuma 88
saucepan 64
saucer 121
sausage 95
savoury bun 93
savoury egg custard 127
saw 118
saxophone 169
scales 80
scallop 99
scanner 144
scarf 116
schoolbag 141
scissors 141
scoreboard 179
scourer 74
screwdriver 118
screws 118
scrub 248
scrum 186
scuba diving 189
sea bass 98
sea bream 98
sea cucumber 99
sea horse 242
seal 242
seatbelt 25
sea urchin 99, 242
seaweed jelly 128
security alarm 56
7-5-3 Festival 256
sewing box 175
sewing machine 175
shamisen 170
shampoo 106
shark 242
sharpener 141
sheep 233
sheet music 170
sheets 69
shiitake mushrooms 91
shin 206
shin pads 185

Shinto shrine 150, 155
shirt 115
shiso 91
shoe cupboard 58
shoe shop 120
Shogi 173
shopping 153
shopping district 78
shorts 115
shot put 199
shoulder 207
shower 70
shower gel 106
showers 181
shrimp 99
shuttlecock 190
sieve 64
SIGHTSEEING 154
sightseeing bus 36, 155
SIM card 137
singer 170
single room 161
sink 65
skateboarding 200
skeleton 209
sketchpad 175
ski boots 193
ski goggles 193
ski helmet 193
ski jacket 193
skijack 97
ski poles 193
skipping rope 181
skirt 115
skis 193
skull 209
sleeping bag 164
sliced loaf 93
sling 220
slippers 58, 117
slug 241
smartphone 137
smoke alarm 56
snail 241
snake 235
snorkelling 189
snowboard 193
snow chains 32
soap 106
socks 115
sofa 61
sole 205
soundbar 168
soy bean paste 81
soy sauce 81, 132
spade 72
spanner 118
spare wheel 32

sparrow 239
spatula 64
speakers 168
speed camera 29
speedometer 25
spiced sake 257
spices 82
spider 241
spikes 199
spinach 91
spine 209
spiny lobster 99
spirits 84
splinter 220
split-toe socks 114
sponge cake 128
spoon 67, 132
sports 153
spray 106
spring onion 91
squash 191
squash ball 191
squash racket 191
squid 99
squirrel 236
stable 234
stadium 179
stamp 148
stands 179
stapler 144
Star Festival 256
starfish 242
stars 249
starting blocks 199
STATION KIOSK 102
station staff 43
stationery 103
steak 95
steamed stuffed bun 134
steering wheel 25
stethoscope 211
sticker 103
sticky notes 144
sticky rice cake 257
sticky tape 144
sting 220
stir-fried Chinese noodles with meat and vegetables 127
stopwatch 199
straw 234
strawberry 88
stream 248
student 141
sudoku 173
sugar 82
suit 115
suitcase 47

263

sumo 197
sumo referee 197
sumo ring 197
sumo wrestler 197
sun 249
sunburn 220
sunflower 244
sunglasses 166
sunhat 166
sunscreen 106, 166
SUPERMARKET AND
  CONVENIENCE
  STORE 79
surfboard 189
surfing 189
sushi 127, 134
swallow 239
swan 239
sweatshirt 115
sweet azuki bean
  soup 128
sweet bun 93
sweetcorn 91
sweetened rice wine
  81
sweetfish 98
sweet potato 91
sweets 83
swimmer 188
swimming cap 188
swimming pool 188
swimming trunks
  166, 188
swimsuit 166, 188
swivel chair 144
syringe 201, 211
table 132
table lamp 61
tablet 106, 137, 201
table tennis 200
taekwondo 197
tail 19, 229
tampon 107
tap 65, 70
tape measure 175
tatami matting 59
taxi 33
TAXIS 33
tea 83
tea bowl 176
tea ceremony 176
tea cup 67

team 179
teapot 64
teaspoon 67
tee 195
teeth 213
telephone 144
tempura 127
tennis 191
tennis ball 191
tennis court 191
tennis player 191
tennis racket 191
tent 151, 164
tent peg 151
tern 239
textbook 141
theatre 158
thermometer 211
thermostat 56
thigh 206
thrush 239
thumb 205
tibia 209
ticket 21
ticket barrier 43
ticket collector 43
ticket machine 43
ticket office 43
tie 116
tiger 237
tights 115
tiles 65
till point 78
TIME 15
timetable 21
tin opener 64
toad 235
toast 124
toasted sandwich
  134
toaster oven 64
toe 205
toenail 205
toiletries 161
toilet roll 70
toll point 29
toll road 28
tomato 91
toothbrush 107
toothpaste 107
toothpicks 132
torch 164

tortoise 235
tour guide 155
tour office 155
tourist office 155
towel 70
tow truck 32
toys 111
toyshop 120
track 43
traditional Chinese
  medicine 226
traffic cone 29
traffic lights 29
train 43
trainers 117
tram 36
travel agency 120
travelling 153
treadmill 181
TREES AND PLANTS
  245
trolley 80
trombone 169
trophy 179
trough 234
trousers 116
trowel 72
trumpet 169
T-shirt 116
tsunami 250
tuba 169
tulip 244
tumble drier 74
tumbler 67
tuna 98
tunnel 29
turntable 168
turtle 235
TV 61
TV stand 61
tweezers 220
twin room 161
typhoon 250
tyre 26, 39
ulna 209
ultrasound 224
umbrella 75
ume plum 88
umpire 191
umpire's chair 191
USB stick 144
vacuum cleaner
  74

valley 248
vase 61
vending machine 134
vertebrae 209
vest 108
VET 227
vet 228
veterinary nurse 228
video game 173
vinegar 81
violet 244
violin 169
virtual reality
  headset 173
volcanic eruption
  250
volleyball 200
wagyu beef 95
waiter 132
waiting room 211
waitress 132
wakame seaweed 81
walking 153
WALKING AND
  CLIMBING 194
walking boots 117,
  194
walking poles 194
wall 56
wallpaper 118
ward 217
wardrobe 69
warning triangle 32
wasabi 81
washing machine 74
washing-up sponge
  62
wasp 241
wastepaper basket
  74
watching TV/films
  153
watercolours 175
waterfall 248
watering can 72
water jug 67
watermelon 88
waterproof jacket
  116
waterskiing 189
WATER SPORTS 187
WEATHER 18

weedkiller 72
weightlifting bench
  181
Wellington boots 117
wet wipes 109
wetsuit 189
whale 242
wheat noodles 81,
  127
wheel 26, 39
wheelbarrow 72
wheelchair 217
whisk 65
whistle 185
white 7
whiteboard 141
white coffee 121, 123
willow 246
window 26, 51, 56
windscreen 26
windscreen wiper 26
windsurfing 189
wine 84
wine glass 67, 132
wing 26, 229
wing mirror 26
WINTER SPORTS 192
wireless router 137
wisteria 246
wok 65
wolf 237
woodblock print 101
wooden clogs 114,
  251
wooden doll 101
wooden spoon 65
woodpecker 239
WORK 13
worktop 65
wrapping paper 78
wrestling 197
wrist 205
writing paper 103
X-ray 217
yacht 50
yellow 7
yellow card 185
yellowtail 98
yoghurt 100, 124
yuzu 88
Zimmer frame® 217

アームバンド 188
合気道 196
アイシャドー 107
アイスクリーム 83, 128
アイスコーヒー 84
アイススケート 193
アイスホッケー 200
アイゼン 194
アイライナー 107
アイロン 74
アイロン台 74
青い 7
赤い 7
赤いピーマン 91
(赤)味噌 81
赤スグリ 88
秋 17
アコースティックギター 168
アコーディオン 168
あご 205
朝ご飯 123
朝顔 244
アサリ 98
アザラシ 242
脚 206
足 205, 206
足のつめ 205
足の裏 205
足の親指 205
足の指 205
足湯 163
アジ 97
アジサシ 239
アスパラガス 89
遊び場 150
頭 206
穴あけパンチ 140
アニメ 157
アパート 51, 53
アヒル 233
油絵具 175
アブラムシ 240
アボカド 86
網棚 43
編み針 174
雨除けシート 151
アメフト 200
アヤメ 243
アユ 98
アリ 240
アルミ箔 62
アロマテラピー 226
(合わせ)味噌 81

泡だて器 65
アワビ 98
アンカー 49
アンコウ 97
安全反射ベスト 32
安全ピン 175
アンパン 92
家 54
家 56
家で食事する 66
イエロー/レッドカード 185
イカ 99
育児 108
イグアナ 235
イグニッション 25
生け花 176
囲碁 173
衣装ダンス 69
移植て 72
椅子 131
伊勢海老 99
イチゴ 88
いちじく 87
市場 85
イチョウ 245
一戸建て 53
糸 174
いなりずし 133
犬 232
犬小屋 234
犬用マットベッド 234
イノシシ 236
居間 60
居間 61
イモムシ 240
イモリ 235
イヤホン 168
イヤリング 116
入り江 49
イルカ 242
入れ歯 213
色鉛筆 139
岩 248
イワシ 98
インクカートリッジ 143
インスタントコーヒー 84
インターホーン 58
インテリア 111
インフレータブル・ミニボート 50
鵜 233
ウィンドサーフィン 189

ウェイター 132
ウェイトレス 132
ウェットスーツ 189
植木鉢 71
ウエットティッシュ 109
ウォーキングと登山 194
ウォータースキー 189
ウォータースポーツ 187
浮世絵 101
ウグイス 239
受け皿 121
受付 161
ウサギ 233
打ち身 219
うちわ 101, 251
腕 206
うどん 81, 127
ウナギ 97, 242
うな重 126
ウニ 99, 242
乳母車 109
馬 233
馬小屋 234
ウミガメ 242
ウミスズメ 239
梅 88
梅干し 81, 124
上着 114
運河 49
運転 26
運転手 33
エアバッグ 32
エアロバイク 191
映画を見ること 153
映画館 150
ATM 146
駅 43
駅のキオスク 102
駅員 43
液剤 105
駅弁 42
エクレア 93
えさ入れ 234
エニシダ 245
絵葉書 148
海老 97
エリザベスカラー 228
エレキギター 169
エレベータ 161
縁側 59
沿岸警備隊ボート 50
エンターテイメント 156
延長コード 55

円盤投げ 198
鉛筆 103, 140
鉛筆削り 141
横断歩道 28
オーケストラ 170
オートバイ 37
オートバイ 37
オーブン 65
オープンースター 64
オール 189
オーロラ 249
オオカミ 232
大型定期船 50
大型手提げかばん 47
大スズメバチ 241
丘 248
(お)会計 78
お粥 124
小川 248
お勘定 130
贈り物 253
贈り物と土産 101
おしぼり 131
お汁粉 128
お節料理 257
おたま 64
お茶／煎茶 84, 124
おちょこ 67, 132
(お)月見 256
お寺 149, 155
おでん 133
お年玉 257
お屠蘇 257
おにぎり 133
(お)花見 256
帯 114
オフィスビル 150
(お)弁当 133
お盆 256
(お)祭り 158
お宮参り 254
おむつ 109
おむつ用クリーム 109
オムレツ 127
(お)餅 257
おもちゃ 111
おもちゃ屋 120
主な食事 125
親子丼 127
親指 205
オリーブオイル 75, 82
折り紙 101, 176
オレンジ 87

オレンジジュース 124
おろし器 63
おわん 66, 131
**音楽** 167
音楽を聞くこと 153
音楽家 170
**温泉** 162
温泉 163
温野菜 127
蚊 241
蛾 241
ガーゼ 220
カーテン 60, 69
カーディガン 114
ガーデニング 153
ガーデニング用手袋 72
カード 103
カードキー 161
カード読取り機 78
カーナビ 25
カーリング 200
カーレース 200
**海洋生物** 242
**海岸** 165
海岸 249
会議場 149
改札口 43
**会社** 142
海水パンツ 166, 188
階段教室 141
懐中電灯 164
回転いす 144
回転寿 168
**外食** 129
ガイドブック 155
買物 153
カイロプラクティック 226
カエデ 246
カエル 235
顔 205
顔 206
かかと 205
鏡 69, 70
カキ 99
柿 88
かき氷 128
かぎ針 174
学食 141
学生 141
学生かばん 141
楽譜 170
家具 111
家具屋 120
崖 249
崖くずれ 250

掛け軸 59
掛け布団 69
かご 75, 80
傘 207
菓子 83, 102
菓子パン 93
歌手 170
**家事** 73
カステラ 128
数独 173
**家族と友だち** 10
ガソリンスタンド 28
肩 207
カタツムリ 241
カッコー 238
滑走路 47
カップ 121
カップと受け皿 66
カツオ 97
鰹節 80
桂 246
カテージチーズ 100
家電 111
家電販売店 119
門松 257
かなづち 118
カナリア 232
カニ 98, 242
カヌー 50
カヌーに乗ること 188
カバ 237
かばん 111
花瓶 59
カフェオーレ 121, 123
歌舞伎 158
カプトムシ 240
カプセル 105
カプセルホテル 161
壁紙 118
かまぼこ 80
紙 140
髪 205
かみそり 106
カメ 235
カメラレンズ 171
鴨肉 95
カモメ 238
カヤック 50
カヤックに乗ること 188
カラオケ 158, 253
辛子 82
カラス 238
**体** 204
体 206, 207

空手 197
カリフラワー 89
カレイ 97
カレーパン 93
カレーライス 126
川 248
皮むき器 64
カワセミ 239
缶切り 64
**飼われている動物と鳥** 231
**観光** 154
観光案内所 155
観光ガイド 155
観光バス 36, 155
看護師 203
監視員 166
環状交差点 29
乾燥機 74
漢方薬 220
観覧席 179
キーウィ 87
キーパーグローブ 185
キーボード 169
黄色い 7
**木とその他の有機体** 245
木のスプーン 65
機関車 42
着替え室 181
貴金属店 120
菊 243
機首 47
喫茶店 149
切手 148
切符 36
切符売場 43
キツツキ 239
キツネ 236
キノコ 90
**基本** 8, 20, 52, 76, 122
着物 113
客室 47
客車 42
キャベツ 89
キャンバス 141
**キャンプ** 164
灸 226
救急救命士 203
救急車 217
救急箱 201, 220
救急絆創膏 106, 201, 220
旧正月 257
きゅうり 66
弓道 197
救命胴衣 50, 189
救命ブイ 50

給油機 28
きゅうり 89
**教育** 138
教会 149
教科書 141
胸骨 209
鏡台 68
切り傷 219
キリン 237
金魚 232
金魚鉢 234
金庫 161
キンポウゲ 243
菌類 245
ギア 39
ギフト 111
牛乳／ミルク 100
餃子 126
行司 197
**銀行** 145
空気入れ 39
くぎ 118
空港 46
草 245
櫛 107
クジラ 242
薬局 203
**果物と野菜** 86
口 205
口紅 107
くちばし 229
クッション 61
クッション封筒 148
靴 120
靴ひも付きの靴 117
靴下 115
靴箱／下駄箱 58
靴屋 120
首 206
クマ 236
熊手 72
熊手 72
クモ 241
雲 249
クラゲ 242
クラゲ 99
クラリネット 168
栗 86, 245
クリーム 100
クリケット 200
くるぶし 205
**車の故障** 30
車椅子 217
クレジットカード 78, 146
黒い 7

クロストレーナー 181
クロワッサン 93, 123
グラタン 127
グランドシート 151
グリーンピース 90
グレープフルーツ 87
グローブ 182
グローブボックス 25
ケーキ 253
脛骨 209
ケージ 228, 233, 234
蛍光ペン 140
警察官 28
警察署 150
計算機 139
掲示板 42
芸術と手工芸 174
係船 50
携帯カバー 137
毛糸(玉) 174
競馬 200
計量カップ 64
競輪 200
ゲートボール 200
ゲーム 172
ゲーム 153
ゲーム機 173
ゲームコントローラ 173
けが 218
劇場 158
ケシ 244
消しゴム 140
化粧品 111, 161
ケチャップ 82
決済箱 143
血圧計 211
ケトルベル 181
煙感知器 56
健康 12
健康飲料 102
健康食品店 120
剣道 197
券売機 43
下駄 114, 251
玄関 57
玄米 80
玄米茶 84
小エビ 99
鯉のぼり 256
コインランドリー 150
コインロッカー 42
公園 150
硬貨 78
交差点 28
講師 141

降車ブザー 36
工事中 29
洪水 250
高速道路 28
紅茶 123
紅茶 83
交番 149
コウモリ 236
ゴーグル 188
コート 114
コート 183
コーヒー 123
コーヒーゼリー 128
コーヒーテーブル 61
コーヒープレス 63
ゴール 177, 185
ゴールキーパー 185
ゴールポスト 186
コオロギ 240
漕ぎ船 50
黒板 139
苔 246
こけし 101
腰 207
こしょう 82, 132
コスプレ 158
こたつ 59
骨格 209
コックピット 19, 47
骨折 219
コップ 131
骨盤 209
小包 148
骨とう品屋 119
琴 170
こどもの日 256
粉ミルク 109
ご飯 126
コピー機 144
こま 1/2
小道 71
ゴミ箱 74
ゴミ袋 74
ゴム手袋 74
米 81
ゴリラ 237
コルク抜き 63
ゴルフ 195
ゴルフカート 195
ゴルフクラブ 195
ゴルフバッグ 195
ゴルフボール 195
ゴルフ練習場 195
コンサート 158
コンタクトレンズ 215

コンタクトレンズケース 215
コンドーム 105
コンパクトカメラ 171
コンパス 194
コンピュータ 136
昆布 81
コロロ 65
サーフィン 189
サーフボード 189
サーモスタット 56
サイ 237
さいころ 173
サイドブレーキ 25
サイドミラー 26
裁判所 150
財布 65
裁縫ばさみ 174
裁縫箱 175
催眠療法 226
サウンドバー 168
魚屋 96
酒瓶 120
サギ 238
サクソフォン 169
桜 245
サケ 97
酒/日本酒 84
鎮骨 209
刺身 127
サッカー 184
サッカー 185
サッカーシューズ 185
サッカー選手 185
サッカーフィールド 177, 185
サッカーボール 185
殺菌クリーム 105
サツマイモ 91
砂糖 82
茶道 176
サドル 39
サバ 97
砂漠 247
サメ 249
さやいんげん 90
皿 67, 131
サラダ 128
サラダボウル 67
サル 237
ざる 64
三角警告板 32
サングラス 166
珊瑚 249
サンゴ礁 249
サンショウウオ 235
酸素マスク 217

サンダル 117
サンドイッチ 133
桟橋 49
散歩 153
サンマ 97
座椅子 59
ザクロ 88
座卓 59, 131
雑誌 102
座布団 59, 131
しいたけ 91
シーツ 69
シートベルト 25
シール 103
ジーンズ 114
指圧 226
塩 82, 132
潮だまり 249
シカ 236
歯科医 213
歯科助手 213
歯科医院 213
歯科用ドリル 213
指揮者 170
仕事 13
刺繍 175
自然災害 250
地すべり 250
しそ 91
下着 111
しっぽ 229
七五三 256
湿地 248
膝蓋骨 209
漆塗り 101
市電/路面電車 36
竹刀 196
市内地図 155
芝刈り機 72
芝生 71
シフトレバー 24
紙幣 78, 146
島 249
SIMカード 137
シャープペン 140
尺八 170
尺骨 209
写真 171
写真 171
車掌 43
車線 28
シャツ 108, 115
シャトル 190
しゃぶしゃぶ 126
シャベル 72

三味線 170
車輪 26, 39
シャワー 70, 181
シャワージェル 106
車両 42
シャンプー 106
ジャガイモ 91, 128
蛇口 65, 70
ジャッキ 32
ジャム 82, 124
市役所 149
獣医 227
獣医 228
獣医看護師 228
祝儀袋 103
修理工 32
じゅうたん 69
柔道 197
修理工場 32
主審 191
手術室 217
出発掲示板 47
シュノーケリング 189
ショウガ 90
将棋 173
錠剤 106, 201
障子 59
ショーツ 115
商店街 78
消防署 150
醤油 81, 132
蒸留酒 84
じょうろ 72
上腕骨 209
食洗器 73
食パン 93
食品 111
食品戸棚 65
ショッピングカート 80
書道 176
シラサギ 238
尻 207
シリアル 123
視力表 215
視力検査 215
歯列矯正器 213
城 155
白い 7
(白)味噌 81
新年 257
新幹線 42
シンク 65
人生の出来事 254
寝具 68
シングルルーム 161

信号 29
診察台 211
寝室 69
寝室 68
身障者用駐車スペース 27
新生児 224
審判台 191
新聞 102
森林 247
森林浴 225
ジェットスキー 188
時間 15
ジグソーパズル 173
時刻表 21
地震 250
自転車 22, 38
自転車 39
自転車ロック 39
自動車 22
自動ドア 33
自動販売機 133
自分について 9
ジムボール 181
宿泊 159
ジョギング 153
ジョギングパンツ 115
助産婦 224
除草剤 72
ジョッキ 130
除夜の鐘 257
神社 150, 155
スーツ 115
スーツケース 47
スーパーとコンビニ 79
酢／米酢 81
水泳する人 188
水泳帽 188
スイカ 88
スイカズラ 246
水彩絵具 175
水槽 233
炊飯器 64
スカート 115
スカッシュ 191
スカッシュボール 191
スカッシュラケット 191
スキー板 193
スキーグローブ 193
スキーゴーグル 193
スキーブーツ 193
スキーヘルメット 193
スキャナ 144
スキューバダイビング 189
杉 245
すき焼き 126

スクラム 186
スクリュー 118
スケート靴 193
スケートボード 200
スケッチブック 175
スコアボード 179
すし 127, 133
スズキ 246
スズキ 98
スズメ 239
スズメバチ 241
スズラン 244
硯 176
スターティングブロック 199
スタジアム 179
ステーキ 95
ストック 193
ストップウォッチ 199
スニーカー 117
すね当て 185
スノーボード 193
スパイク 199
スパイス 82
スパッツ 115
スパナ 118
スピーカー 168
スピードカメラ 29
スプーン 67, 132
スプレー 106
スペアリブ 95
スポーツ 183
スポンジ 62
スマートフォン 137
墨 176
墨絵 176
スミレ 244
相撲 197
相撲取り 197
擦り傷 219
スリッパ 58, 117
頭蓋骨 209
ズッキーニ 89
ズボン 116
セーター 115
制汗剤 106
整骨療法 226
(生理用)ナプキン 106
セキセイインコ 232
脊柱 209
咳止め 105
咳止めドロップ 106
石鹸 106
背中 207
セミ 240

セロテープ™ 144
セロリ 89
洗車 28
線審 185, 191
扇子 101
センターサークル 177
洗濯かご 69
洗濯ばさみ 73
洗濯機 74
扇風機 60
せんべい 83
線路 43
ゼムクリップ 144
ゾウ 237
雑木林 248
雑巾 62
装飾品 111
掃除機 74
速度計 25
ソファー 61
その他 119
その他のスポーツ 200
袖 80, 126
空の旅 44
そろばん 140
鯛 98
体温計 211
太鼓 170
大根 90
体操 200
大聖堂 155
代替療法 225
台所 62
台所 65
ダイバー 188
タイツ 115
体内 208
台風 250
タイヤ 26, 39
タイヤチェーン 32
太陽 249
タイル 65
タオル 70
滝 248
タクシー 33
タクシー 33
竹 245
タケノコ 89
タコ 99
たこやき 133
だし 80
畳 59

抱っこひも 109
卓球 200
ダッシュボード 24
タツノオトシゴ 242
七夕 256
谷 248
タヌキ 236
タバコ 102
足袋 114
タブレット 137
ダブルベース 168
ダブルルーム 161
卵 100
卵焼き 124
タマネギ 90
タラ 97
タラップ 49
だるま 101
炭酸ドリンク 84
タンス 69
タンブラー 67
タンポポ 243
タンポン 107
団子 83
団地 53
ダンベル 181
**小さい生き物 240**
チーター 237
チーム 179
地衣類 246
チェーン 39
チェス 172
チェダーチーズ 100
チェリー 86
チェロ 168
地下鉄 43
チケット 21, 36
地図 21
チャージャー 136
茶の湯／茶道 176
チャイルドシート 109
茶碗 67, 132, 176
茶碗蒸し 127
ちゃんこ鍋 126
チューバ 169
チューリップ 244
中華鍋 65
注射器 201
注射器 211
駐車場 5
駐車スペース 28
チョウ 240
超音波 224
長距離バス 36
聴診器 211

**朝食 123**
調理台 65
貯金通帳 146
チョコレート 83, 253
ちり取り 74
チンゲン菜 90
椎骨 209
ツインルーム 161
**通信とIT 135**
月 249
机 143
ツグミ 239
漬物 81
ツタ 246
鼓 170
津波 250
椿 245
翼 229
ツバメ 239
つまようじ 132
つめ 229
爪 229
梅雨 17
吊り包帯 220
ツル 238
鶴 229
手 205, 206
テーブル 132
ティー 195
ティースプーン 67
Tシャツ 119
ティーポット 64
DVDプレイヤー 60
手押し車 72
手紙 148
手首 205
テコンドー 197
**鉄道 40**
デジカメ 171
テニス 191
テニスのボール 191
テニスコート 191
テニス選手 191
テニスラケット 191
手荷物受取 46
手荷物カート 47
手ぬぐい 70, 101
手のひら 205
手の指 205
手袋 116
テレビ 61
映画を見ること 153
テレビ台 61
**天気 18**
転職 254

点滴 217
テント 151, 164
テントウ虫 241
テントペグ 151
テントロープ 151
天パン 63
デジタルカメラ 171
デニッシュペストリー 93
**デパート 110**
デビットカード 78, 146
電気スタンド 61, 143
電気屋 119
電球 56
電車 43
電子レンジ 65
デンタルフロス 107
臀部 207
てんぷら 127
電話 144
ドア 26
ドアスコープ 58
道路 28
トースト 124
ドーナツ 93
とい 56
とう骨 209
ドクターヘリ 217
とげ 220
ところてん 128
とっくり 67
どら焼き 83
トイレットペーパー 70
トイレトレー 234
トウガラシ 89
陶芸 175
搭乗券 47
搭乗手続きカウンター 47
豆腐 80
トウモロコシ 91
灯籠流し 256
トカゲ 235
読書 153
床屋 119
図書館 141, 150
取手 121
トップチューブ 39
トナカイ 237
飛込み台 188
土俵 197
トマト 91
トラ 237
ドライバー 118
ドライヤー 69
トラック 199
ドラム 169

ドレス 114
ドレッサー 68
トランク 26
トランプ 172
トランペット 169
**鳥 238**
トレーナー 115
トレッキングシューズ 117
トレッキングシューズ 194
トレッキングポール 194
トロフィー 179
トロンボーン 169
トンカツ 126
トンネル 29
トンビ 238
トンボ 241
ナイフ 66, 131
ナイロンたわし 74
長靴 117
梨 87
ナス 89
夏 17
ナッツ 83
納豆 80, 124
ナプキン 67
鍋 64
なまこ 99
生野菜 122
ナメクジ 241
納屋 233
縄跳び 181
軟膏 220
ナンバープレート 26
肉hands(みそ) 133
**肉屋 94**
ニシン 97
虹 249
ニジマス 97
二段ベッド 68
**日、月、季節 16**
**日曜大工 118**
日曜大工 153
**日本の部屋 59**
日本の民族衣装 251
**乳製品 100**
庭 71
庭 71, 233
鶏 233
人形 101
**妊娠 223**
妊娠検査 224
ニンジン 89
ニンニク 90
布 174
ネーブル 87

ネギ 91
ネクタイ 116
ネクタリン 87
猫 232
ネズミ 236
ネックレス 116
熱 222
寝袋 164
年賀状 257
燃料計 24
ノート 103
ノートパソコン 144
能 158
農家 53
野ウサギ 236
農地 247
のこぎり 118
のれん 163
ノスリ 238
ノミよけ首輪 228
海苔 81
歯 213
バー 157
バーガー 95, 133
パーティー 253
ハードル 199
ハーブ 82
ハーブ療法 226
ハープ 169
バイオリン 169
灰皿 130
パイソン 236
バインダー 140
歯医者 213
歯医者の椅子 213
排水管 56
ハイチェア 109
パイナップル 88
ハイヒール 117
パイロット 47
ハエ 241
葉書き 103
はかり 80
バケツ 73
はさみ 72, 141
はっぴ 113
吐き気 222
白菜 89
白鳥 239
博物館 155
歯茎 213
箱 148
橋 27
箸 66, 131
箸置き 66, 131

パジャマ 115
走り高跳び 198
走り幅跳び 199
バス 36
バスターミナル 36
バス停 36
**バスと市電 34**
**バスケットボール 183**
バスケット 183
バスケット(ボール) 183
バスケットのボール 183
バスケットシューズ 183
バスケット選手 183
パスタ 82, 127
パスポート 47
肌着 111
ハチミツ 82
バックミラー 25
発疹 222
初詣 257
バット 182
ハト 238
バドミントン 190
バドミントンラケット 190
パドル 189
パドルボード 189
**花 243**
花 71, 176
鼻 205
花束 253
バナナ 75, 86
花火 253
花屋 120
パパイヤ 88
歯ブラシ 107
歯磨き粉 107
ハム 95
ハムスター 233
ハモニカ 169
腹 206
バラ 244
鍼 226
針 174
ハリネズミ 236
春 17
バレーボール 200
ハンガー 68
帆船 50, 189
絆創膏 222
バンパー 26
半島 249
ハンドバッグ 116
ハンドミキサー 63
ハンドル 25

ハンドル 39
初宮参り 254
パン 75, 123
パンジー 244
パンツ 114, 116
パンティー 115
パンプス 117
**パン屋 92**
ピアノ 169
ヒーター 56
挽いたコーヒー 84
ビーチサンダル 166
ビーチボール 166
ビール 83
ヒキガエル 235
引き出し 65, 69
ビキニ 166
飛行機 46
膝プロテクター 37
ひじ 207
肘掛け椅子 61
ひじき 80
ひ骨 209
非常電話 32
美術館 155
額 205
羊 233
ピッケル 194
ビデオゲーム 173
ヒトデ 240
ヒナギク 243
ヒバリ 239
尾部 19
ヒマワリ 244
びわ 87
100円ショップ 119
日焼けの炎症 220
日焼け止め 106, 166
ヒューズボックス 55
ヒョウ 237
**病院 216**
病院 150, 203
美容院 120
**病院の予約 210**
病院ベッド 217
氷河 248
**病気 221**
病棟 217
氷のう 220
表彰台 179
ヒラメ 97
琵琶 170
ピンセット 220
便せん 103

ブイ 49
VR ヘッドセット 173
フードプロセッサー 63
**ファーストフード 133**
ファイリングキャビネット 143
ファッション 111
ファンデーション 107
**フィットネス 180**
フィンチ 238
ブースターケーブル 32
ブーツ 37, 117
封筒 103, 148
フェリー 50
**フェリーと船の旅 48**
フェンダー 26
フォーク 66, 131
フォルダー 143
**服 112**
ふくらはぎ 207
フクロウ 239
藤 246
**武術と相撲 196**
付箋 144
豚 233
ブドウ 87
筆 176
不凍液 32
ブドウの木 245
布団 59
冬 17
**冬のスポーツ 192**
踏切 28
フライ返し 63
フライド慈し 127
フライドポテト 127
フライパン 63
フランスパン 92
フルーツジュース 84
フルーツパフェ 128
フルート 169
ブルーレイプレヤー 60
フルフェイス・ヘルメット 37
フレーム 39, 215
フレンチフライ 133
**風呂 70**
風呂 70
風呂イス 163
フロントガラス 26
噴火 250
ブラ 114
ブラインド 60
ブラウス 114
ブラシ 73
ブリ 98
ブリオッシュ 93

ブルーチーズ 100
ブルートゥーススピーカー 168
ブルートゥース™ヘッドセット 136
ブルーベリー 86
ブレーキ 39
ブレード 19
ブレスレット 116
ブロッコリー 89
**文具店** 103
分娩室 224
文房具 103
文楽 158
プール 188
プリン 128
プリンター 144
ヘアブラシ 107
塀 56, 71
ベーコン 95
ベースギター 168
ペーパータオル 62
ペダル 39
ペダルビン 62
ベッド 69
ベッドサイドテーブル 69
ペットショップ 120
ペットフード 234
ヘッドホン 168
ヘッドライト 26
ヘッドランプ 39
ヘッドレスト 25
ベナルティーボックス 177
ヘビ 235
ベビーカー 109
ベビーシューズ 108
ベビーバッグ 108
ベビーフード 108
ベビーベッド 109
へら 64
ベランダ 51, 56
ヘリコプター 19
ベル 39
ベルト 116
ヘルメット 39
ベンチプレス 181
ペン 102, 140
ペンキ 118
ペンキブラシ 118
ペンギン 239
ペンケース 140
ホース 72
ホーム 43
保育器 224

ホイッスル 185
ボイラー 55
砲丸投げ 199
方向指示器 26
帽子 108
包装紙 78
包帯 105, 201, 220
包丁 63
ほうじ茶 84
忘年会 257
防犯警報装置 56
ほうれん草 91
ボウル 64
ほお 205
ほお紅 107
ボールガール 191
ボールボーイ 191
防水ジャケット 116
棒高跳び 199
ボクシング 196
牧草地 234
歩行補助器 217
星 249
干し草 234
ホステル 161
ホタテ貝 99
蛍 241
ホチキス™ 141
ボタン 174
ボタン 244
ホットケーキ 93
ホットサンド 133
ホットドッグ 133
ポップコーン 83
ポテトチップス 83
ホテル 53, 150
歩道 28
哺乳瓶 108
**ほ乳類** 236
ホワイトボード 141
本棚 61
本屋 119
盆栽 176
盆栽ばさみ 72
ボンネット 26
マイクロバス 36
舞子 157
マウスパッド 137
巻きずし 133
枕 69
マグロ 98
マスカラ 107
**町で** 149
待合室 211
待ち針 175

マッサージ 226
マッシュルーム 90
抹茶 84
マットレス 69
マツ 246
松葉づえ 217
**祭り** 255
窓 26, 51, 56
窓シャッター 56
まな板 53
マニキュア 107
マフラー 116
まめ 219
マヨネーズ 82
まわし 197
マンゴー 87
マンション 51, 53
みかん 88
みそ汁 124, 126
ミシン 175
水きりボウル 63
湖 248
水切り台 65
水着 166, 188
水差し 67
ミツバチ 240
ミトン 108
緑の 7
ミニバー 161
ミネラルウォーター 84
耳 205
ミミズ 241
ミュージカル 158
ミュージシャン 170
ミュージックショップ 120
味醂 81
ミンチ 95
ムール貝 99
ムカデ 240
麦茶 83
麦わら帽子 166
むこうずね 206
虫よけ 106
虫刺され 220
無線ルーター 137
胸 206
目 205
メーター 56
瞑想 226
雌牛 233
眼鏡 215
眼鏡ケース 215
**眼鏡屋** 214
眼鏡屋 120, 215
目薬 215

目覚まし時計 68
メジャー 175
メダル 179
メニュー 131
メモ帳 144
メロン 87
免税店 47
綿棒 109
めん棒 64
毛布 68
模型作り 175
モスク 150
モップ 74
モツァレラ 100
モニター 217
物差し 140
物干し 73
物干しざお 74
モーレル 43
モバイルパワーパック 137
モミ 245
紅葉狩り 256
モモ 88
腿 206
モルモット 232
門 56
やかん 63
焼き魚 124
焼きそば 127
焼き鳥 133
**野球** 182
野球 182
野球のボール 182
野球選手 182
野球帽 182
ヤギ 233
薬剤師 203
火傷 219
**薬局** 104
薬局 203
ヤナギ 246
屋根 51
屋根 26
屋根 56
山 248
ヤモリ 235
やり投げ 199
USB メモリ 144
遊園地 158
郵便受け 56
**郵便局** 147
郵便局員 148
郵便ポスト 148
床 61
浴衣 113, 163, 251

ゆず 88
ゆで卵 124
湯呑茶碗 67, 131
指関節 205
ユリ 244
ようかん 128
ヨーグルト 100
ヨーグルト 124
幼児用おまる 109
浴槽 70
よだれ掛け 108
ヨット 50
呼び鈴 58
予備タイヤ 32
ラーメン 80, 126
ライオン 237
落語 158
ラクダ 236
**ラグビー** 186
ラグビー 186
ラグビー選手 186
ラグビー場 186
ラグビーボール 186

**ラケット** 190
ラジオ 60
ラッパズイセン 243
ラップ 62
ラップトップ 144
ラベンダー 244
ラン 244
ランドセル 141
ランニングマシーン 181
リーキー 90
リード 228
**陸、海、空** 247
**陸上競技** 198
陸上競技の選手 198
リス 236
リフレクソロジー 226
リフレクター 39
リモコン 60
両替所 146
両替率 146
料金所 29
**両生類とは虫類** 235
料理 153

旅館 53, 161
旅行 153
旅行代理店 120
リンゴ 86
冷凍冷蔵庫 65
レザーカーテン 37
レザージャケット 37
レシート 78
レジ袋 78
レジャーセンター 179
レスリング 197
レタス 90
レッカー車 32
レフェリー 179
レモン 87
レモンソール 97
レンコン 90
練習帳 140
レントゲン 217
ローイングマシーン 181
ローター 19
ロードコーン 29
ロープ 194

ロールパン 92
廊下 161
ロッカー 181
肋骨 209
露天風呂 163
ロブスター 99, 242
路面電車 36
ロンパース 108
ワイパー 26
ワイン 84
ワイングラス 67, 132
和傘 101
ワカメ 81
和菓子 176
和牛 95
わさび 81
ワシ 238
和紙 176
ワニ 235
わら 234
ワンピース 114

## PHOTO CREDITS